BOUNDARIES
with Kids

Resources by Henry Cloud and John Townsend

Boundaries

Boundaries Workbook

Boundaries audio

Boundaries curriculum

Boundaries in Dating

Boundaries in Dating Workbook

Boundaries in Dating audio

Boundaries in Dating curriculum

Boundaries in Marriage

Boundaries in Marriage Workbook

Boundaries in Marriage audio

Boundaries in Marriage curriculum

Boundaries with Kids

Boundaries with Kids Workbook

Boundaries with Kids audio

Boundaries with Kids curriculum

Changes That Heal (Cloud)

Changes That Heal Workbook (Cloud)

Changes That Heal audio (Cloud)

Hiding from Love (Townsend)

How People Grow

How People Grow Workbook

How People Grow audio

How to Have That Difficult Conversation You've Been Avoiding

Making Small Groups Work

Making Small Groups Work audio

The Mom Factor

The Mom Factor Workbook

Raising Great Kids

Raising Great Kids audio

Raising Great Kids for Parents of Preschoolers curriculum

Raising Great Kids Workbook for Parents of Preschoolers

Raising Great Kids Workbook for Parents of School-Age Children

Raising Great Kids Workbook for Parents of Teenagers

Safe People

Safe People Workbook

12 "Christian" Beliefs That Can Drive You Crazy

BOUNDARIES
with Kids

Leader's Guide

When to Say YES,
When to Say NO,
to Help Your Children
Gain Control of Their Lives

Dr. Henry Cloud
Dr. John Townsend

with Lisa Guest

ZONDERVAN®

ZONDERVAN.com/
AUTHORTRACKER
follow your favorite authors

Boundaries with Kids Leader's Guide
Copyright © 2002 by Henry Cloud and John Townsend
Requests for information should be addressed to:

Zondervan, Grand Rapids, Michigan 49530

ISBN-10: 0-310-24724-1
ISBN-13: 978-0-310-24724-1

Published in association with Yates & Yates, LLP, Attorneys and Counselors, Suite 1000, Literary Agent, Orange, CA.

Interior design by Rob Monacelli

*Printed in the United States of America*1

To all those who want to help their children become
the adults that God intended them to be

CONTENTS

The Relentless but Rewarding Task of Parenting   9

Laying the Foundation   11
  This Kit Contains   11
  How This Leader's Guide Is Organized   11
  A Note about Timing   13
  Before the First Session   13
  Five Tips for Leading Group Discussion   13

SESSION 1
Building Character in Kids   15

SESSION 2
Kids Need Parents with Boundaries   31

SESSION 3
*Boundary Principles One and Two: The Law of Sowing and
Reaping and the Law of Responsibility*   47

SESSION 4
*Boundary Principles Three and Four:
The Laws of Power and Respect*   65

SESSION 5
*Boundary Principles Five and Six:
The Laws of Motivation and Evaluation*   85

SESSION 6
*Boundary Principles Seven and Eight:
The Laws of Proactivity Envy*   101

SESSION 7
*Boundary Principles Nine and Ten:
The Laws of Activity and Exposure*   117

SESSION 8
Six Steps to Implementing Boundaries with Your Kids   133

The Relentless But Rewarding Task of Parenting

A wise friend once rightly observed that parenting is relentless. Indeed, the task of helping children develop inside them what you, their parents, have been providing on the outside—responsibility, self-control, and freedom—is not an easy one. But, based on our clinical training and our more than twenty years of working with families, *Boundaries with Kids* can help.

We have organized this curriculum around key concepts that will help children take ownership of their lives. These principles arise from our study of the Bible and God's teaching on responsibility, stewardship, and self-control. We believe these principles of boundaries with children are universal, and that they work with kids at all levels of development. We'll offer some examples and illustrations of how those laws are applied at all age levels, and in the Participant's Guide you will apply these principles to your own parenting situation.

As you lead, keep in mind—and remind the participants if necessary—that *Boundaries with Kids* is geared much more toward how they, the parents, behave with their child than toward educating their child. Learning boundaries has a lot to do with going through experiences such as receiving consequences for behavior, taking ownership, and dealing with the boundaries of others. As parents learn to require responsibility from their child, their child will learn the value of being responsible. The boundary-building process begins with the parents.

Parents are not in this alone. God is also a parent and for many years has gone through the same pains we parents are experiencing as we try to teach responsibility to the kids in our life. God understands, and he will guide and help our willing heart (Psalm 1:6). Encourage your group to ask God for his help, wisdom, and resources as they help their children grow up into maturity in him.

Henry Cloud, Ph.D.
John Townsend, Ph.D.

Laying the Foundation

THIS KIT CONTAINS

- *Boundaries with Kids*—In this best-seller, Dr. Henry Cloud and Dr. John Townsend help you prepare your kids to assume responsibility for their own lives. They show you how to bring control to an out-of-control family life, how to set limits and still be a loving parent, how to define legitimate boundaries for your family, and, above all, how to instill in your children the kind of godly character that is the foundation for healthy, productive adult living.

- *Boundaries with Kids* Video—This eight-part video features the wisdom and insights of Drs. Cloud and Townsend. Interspersed are helpful real-life vignettes of parents learning to apply the ten laws of boundaries to parenting so their children will develop self-control and godly character.

- *Boundaries with Kids Leader's Guide*—This comprehensive, user-friendly guide provides information to help you lead your group through the eight sessions of this course.

- *Boundaries with Kids Participant's Guide*—This guide provides valuable notes and practical exercises (small group discussion starters, questions to help parents and their kids establish and respect boundaries, etc.) that will help you apply to your own life the principles you learn.

Additional kits and copies of the Participant's Guide are available from:

Zondervan
5300 Patterson Avenue SE
Grand Rapids, MI 49530
Phone 1-800-727-3480

HOW THIS LEADER'S GUIDE IS ORGANIZED

The *Boundaries with Kids* course is divided into eight sessions ranging in length from 45–50 minutes. This guide walks you through each session to help you prepare. You will also rely on this guide during the sessions, when you'll find the pages reprinted from the Participant's Guide very helpful.

Each session is divided into four parts: Before You Lead, Introduction, Discovery, and Wrap-up.

Before You Lead

Key Points is a list of the session's main ideas.

The **Synopsis** is a more detailed overview of the session's main points.

The **Session Outline** lists the elements of the meeting.

Recommended Reading encourages you to read the corresponding chapter(s) of Dr. Cloud and Dr. Townsend's book *Boundaries with Kids* in preparation for each session.

Introduction

The Introduction includes calling the class together, welcoming them, and opening in prayer.

Discovery

The session material is found on the left-hand page of the Leader's Guide. You may want to read the material word for word, or you might prefer to highlight the key words and phrases. Get to know the participants and let them get to know you a little. Make your teaching personal.

On the right-hand page is a copy of the corresponding Participant's Guide page(s). There is also space on this right-hand page for you to write in any additional planning notes. Having the corresponding Participant's Guide page in front of you allows you to view the page the participants are seeing as you talk without having to hold two books at the same time. It also lets you know where the participants are in their book when someone asks a question.

The Discovery section also includes the following key typographical elements:

1. The instructor narrative is shown in standard typeface.

2. Directions to the instructor are enclosed in a shaded box and are not meant to be spoken.

3. Occasionally you'll find statements which you should read verbatim. These statements (set off with an arrow) correlate to statements also included in the Participant's Guide.

Video Segments: Each of the sessions has at least two corresponding video clips. The content of each clip is shown in italics for the leader's information, and there is a corresponding page in the Participant's Guide for notes. The video portion of the session will provide a springboard for class discussion and activities.

Exercises: Exercises will be done either alone, in small groups, or with the group as a whole. Directions are included for each exercise. This material is also included in the Participant's Guide.

Wrap-up

Each session closes with a prayer which highlights session themes.

A Note about Timing

Depending on your particular setting, you can lengthen or shorten each session to accommodate your group. Be aware that discussion times may run longer or shorter than what you plan. Try to have an alternate plan for each session: know where you can cut time or add an additional discussion question or two.

Before the First Session

- If desired, use the promotional segment provided on the *Boundaries with Kids Video* to generate interest a few weeks before you begin.

- Read the first two chapters of *Boundaries with Kids* and go over the entire plan for the first session, as outlined in the Leader's Guide.

- Watch the session's video material.

- Obtain a Participant's Guide for each participant. Consider also having available for purchase copies of *Boundaries with Kids* and the *Boundaries with Kids Workbook*, both by Dr. Henry Cloud and Dr. John Townsend.

- Make sure you have all the items listed below:

  For each session, the *leader* will use:

  > Leader's Guide
  > Bible
  > *Boundaries with Kids* by Dr. Henry Cloud and Dr. John Townsend
  > Video (or DVD) player, monitor, stand, extension cord, etc.
  > Videotape (or DVD)

  For each session, the *participants* will use:

  > Participant's Guide
  > Bible
  > Pen or pencil
  > *Boundaries with Kids* by Dr. Henry Cloud and Dr. John Townsend (optional)
  > *Boundaries with Kids Workbook* by Dr. Henry Cloud and Dr. John Townsend (optional)

Five Tips for Leading Group Discussion

1. Allow group members to participate at their own comfort level. Don't require everyone to answer every question.

2. Ask questions with interest and warmth and then listen carefully to individual responses. Remember: no answer is insignificant. Encourage and affirm each person's participation.

3. Be flexible. Reword questions if necessary. Take the liberty of adding or deleting questions to accommodate your group members.

4. Allow for (and expect) differences of opinion and experience.

5. DO NOT BE AFRAID OF SILENCE! Allow people time to think—don't panic! Sometimes ten seconds of silence seems like an eternity. Some of this material is difficult to process. Allow people time to digest the question and then respond.

Session One

Building Character in Kids

BEFORE YOU LEAD

Key Points

- One goal of parenting is to keep an eye on the future. We are raising our children to be responsible adults.

- A person's character is one's destiny, and healthy boundaries can go far in developing character that will lead your children into the life God created them to have.

- A boundary is a "property line" that defines a person; it defines where one person ends and someone else begins.

- The parent or caretaker role consists of three main functions: guardian, manager, and source.

- A guardian is legally responsible for a child and, in that capacity, protects and preserves the child.

- A manager makes sure things get done—goals are reached, demands and expectations are met.

- Parents are the source of all good things (material and immaterial) for a child. They progressively give children the independence to obtain what they need on their own.

- Boundaries facilitate the process of having the child internalize things (feeling the need or motivation to take responsibility for himself, planning for and taking the time to act responsibly, developing the skills necessary to act responsibly) that were previously external to him.

- We want our children to be loving, responsible, free, initiating, respectful of reality, growing, oriented to truth, and oriented to transcendence. These eight qualities are important to adult functioning, and boundaries play an essential developmental role.

Synopsis

One goal of parenting is to keep an eye on the future. We are raising our children to be responsible adults. The issue in any parenting situation is this: *Is what you are doing being done on purpose?*

Parenting has to do with more than the present. You are parenting your child for the future. A person's character is one's destiny, and healthy boundaries can go far in developing character that will lead your children into the life God created them to have.

A boundary is a "property line" that defines a person; it defines where one person ends and someone else begins. If we know where a person's boundaries are, we know that we can expect this person to take control of himself or herself. We can require responsibility in regard to feelings, behaviors, and attitudes.

A child needs to know where she begins, what she needs to take responsibility for, and what she does not need to take responsibility for. When boundaries are clear, children develop a well-defined sense of who they are and what they are responsible for; the ability to choose; the understanding that if they choose well, things will go well and if they choose poorly, they will suffer; and the possibility of true love based in freedom. Self-control, responsibility, freedom, and love—what could be a better outcome of parenting than that?

But how does this transformation occur? We believe that the parent or caretaker role consists of three main functions, that of guardian, manager, and source. A guardian is legally responsible for a child and, in that capacity, protects and preserves the child. In this capacity, parents set limits to freedom and then enforce them for the child's protection. Through this process, the child internalizes the limits as wisdom and slowly begins to be able to take care of herself.

A manager makes sure things get done—that goals are reached, demands and expectations are met. Children are not born with self-discipline; therefore they have to be given "other-discipline." Boundaries play an important role in managing. Setting limits and requiring the child to take ownership (embracing the problem as his own) and responsibility (taking care of what he has embraced) entail a clear understanding of boundaries.

Parents are the source of all good things (material and immaterial) for a child. They are the bridge to the outside world of resources that sustain life. In both giving and receiving resources, boundaries play an important role. As boundaries are learned, parents can progressively give children the independence to obtain what they need on their own.

Boundaries facilitate the process of having the child internalize things (feeling the need or motivation to take responsibility for himself, planning for and taking the time to act responsibly, developing the skills necessary to act responsibly) that were previously external to him.

As you take a stance of clear boundaries with children, they will have a better chance of gaining the motivation, the need, the skill, and the plan to live a loving, responsible, righteous, and successful life unto God and others. And this is what character is all about.

We want our children to be loving, responsible, free, initiating, respectful of reality, growing, oriented to truth, and oriented to transcendence. These eight qualities are important to adult functioning, and boundaries play an essential developmental role. Seeing character building as a task of parenting can be overwhelming, but it cannot be stressed enough, as a child's character will determine much of the course his life takes.

Session Outline (50 minutes)

    I. Introduction (10 minutes)
       A. Welcome (8 minutes)
       B. Overview (1 minute)
       C. Opening Prayer (1 minute)
    II. Discovery (39 minutes)
       A. Video Segment: Parenting with an Eye to the Future (5 minutes)
       B. Kid Talk: What's a Mom to Do? (10 minutes)
       C. Kid Kare: The Parent as Guardian, Manager, and Source (10 minutes)
       D. Video Segment: Eight Key Aspects of Character (6 minutes)
       E. Kid Kare: Cultivating Character (8 minutes)
    III. Wrap-up (1 minute)

Recommended Reading

"The Future Is Now" and "What Does Character Look Like?" chapters 1 and 2 in *Boundaries with Kids*.

Session One

Building Character in Kids

10 MINUTES INTRODUCTION

9 minutes   *Welcome*

> Call the group together and welcome the participants to Session 1 of Boundaries with Kids: Building Character in Kids. Introduce yourself: Tell the group your name and a little about yourself, including the role you play in kids' lives, the number of kids and grandkids you have, etc.

To get to know each other a bit, please turn to page 11 of your Participant's Guide. There you'll see two questions I'd like each of you to answer briefly as we go around the room and introduce ourselves.

> Take 8 minutes to go around the room. Note: If the group is too big, have participants break into groups of three or four.

1 minute   *Overview*

> Participant's Guide page 12.
>
> Note: On each facing right-hand page is a copy of the corresponding Participant's Guide page(s).

Thanks! Now, let's talk a little bit about this course. It is based on Dr. Henry Cloud and Dr. John Townsend's best-selling book *Boundaries with Kids*.

> Hold up a copy of *Boundaries with Kids*. At this point you may wish to offer the book for sale as an additional resource or simply mention where a copy can be obtained.

PLANNING NOTES

_____

_____

_____

_____

_____

_____

_____

_____

_____

_____

_____

_____

_____

_____

_____

_____

_____

_____

_____

_____

_____

_____

_____

_____

_____

_____

_____

Session One — Building Character in Kids

BEFORE WE START

1. What role(s) do you play in kids' lives?

Parent	Daycare worker
Teacher	Babysitter or nanny
Grandparent	Church youth worker
Coach	Sunday school teacher
Neighbor	Other:

2. What do you hope to gain from this course? Put differently, which of the following, if any, are currently issues involving the kid(s) in your life?

Impulsivity	Aggressive behavior
School problems	Conflicts with friends
Defying authority	Sexual involvement
Whining	Drugs
Procrastination	Gangs
Inability to finish tasks	Inattention to parental directives

   Things are going well— and I want to keep it that way!

11

---

12   *Boundaries with Kids Participant's Guide*

OVERVIEW

In this session, you will

- Consider that parenting is best done with an eye to the future.

- Look at three aspects of a parent's role: guardian, manager, and source.

- Be introduced to the concept of boundaries.

- Begin to see the role boundaries can play in giving kids the motivation, the skills, and a plan for living a loving, responsible, righteous, and successful life unto God and others.

- Explore eight key aspects of character. We want our children to be loving, responsible, free, initiating, respectful of reality, growing, oriented to truth, and oriented to transcendence.

In these eight sessions, we are going to look at boundaries with kids. This course is designed to help you consider what boundaries are and the role they can play in building character in kids. In each session, you will be viewing two video segments in which you'll hear Dr. Cloud and Dr. Townsend teach key points from the book. You will discuss various topics as a large group. You will also meet together in small groups, and sometimes work alone on an exercise. Your Participant's Guide will help you stay focused and keep us moving through the material.

Please turn to page 12.

➜ Today we'll be called to parent with an eye to the future. We'll also be introduced to the concept of boundaries and the way that parents—functioning as guardians, managers, and the source of good things—can use boundaries to give kids the motivation, the skills, and a plan for living a loving, responsible, and successful life unto God and others.

Before we go any further, let's open with a word of prayer.

1 minute   *Opening Prayer*

Lord God, thank you for the privilege of being parents, the privilege of being involved in kids' lives. That wonderful privilege, however, carries with it not only much joy but lots of responsibility and countless challenges as well. We come before you today to ask for wisdom and creativity, for renewed hope and energy, as we consider how you might use us effectively in kids' lives. We look forward to what we'll learn and thank you in advance for blessing our efforts to be good stewards of the kids you have placed in our lives. We pray in Jesus' name. Amen.

39 MINUTES DISCOVERY

5 minutes   *Video Segment: Parenting with an Eye to the Future*

> Participant's Guide page 13–14.

In the opening of this first video segment, you will hear Dr. Cloud and Dr. Townsend define boundaries, discuss the benefits of setting clear boundaries with kids, and outline three main capacities in which parents and caretakers function to develop self-control, responsibility, freedom, and love in kids.

Turn to pages 13 and 14 and you'll see that the authors have listed the key points from the video segment so you don't have to take notes while

PLANNING NOTES

_____

_____

_____

_____

_____

_____

_____

_____

_____

_____

_____

_____

_____

_____

_____

_____

_____

OVERVIEW

In this session, you will

- Consider that parenting is best done with an eye to the future.
- Look at three aspects of a parent's role: guardian, manager, and source.
- Be introduced to the concept of boundaries.
- Begin to see the role boundaries can play in giving kids the motivation, the skills, and a plan for living a loving, responsible, righteous, and successful life unto God and others.
- Explore eight key aspects of character. We want our children to be loving, responsible, free, initiating, respectful of reality, growing, oriented to truth, and oriented to transcendence.

VIDEO SEGMENT

Parenting with an Eye to the Future

- One goal of parenting is to keep an eye on the future. We are raising our children to be responsible adults.

- The issue in any parenting situation is this: Is what you are doing being done on purpose? Or are you doing it from reasons that you do not think about, such as your childhood, the need of the moment, your fears, or your own personality?

- A person's character is one's destiny. *Boundaries with Kids* can assist you in helping your children develop the character that will lead them into the life that God created for them.

- A boundary is a "property line" that defines where one person ends and someone else begins. If we know where a person's boundaries are, we know that we can expect this person to take control of himself or herself. We can require responsibility in regard to feelings, behaviors, and attitudes.

- When boundaries are clear, children develop a well-defined sense of who they are and what they are responsible for; the ability to choose; the understanding that if they choose well, things will go well and that if they choose poorly, they will suffer; and the possibility of true love based in freedom. Self-control, responsibility, freedom, and love—what could be a better outcome of parenting than that?

- But how does a child develop these characteristics? It happens as the parent or caretaker acts in three main capacities: that of guardian, manager, and source.

- A guardian is legally responsible for a child and, in that capacity, protects and preserves the child. More often than not in their role as guardian, parents use boundaries to keep their child safe, growing, and healthy. They set limits to freedom and then enforce them for the child's protection. Through this process, the child internalizes the limits as wisdom and slowly begins to be able to take care of herself.

- A manager makes sure things get done—that goals are reached, demands and expectations are met. Children are not born with self-discipline; therefore they have to have "other-discipline." Boundaries play an important role in managing a child. Setting limits and requiring the child to take ownership (embracing the problem as his own) and responsibility (taking care of what he has embraced) entail a clear understanding of boundaries from the parent.

- Parents are the source of all good things (material and immaterial) for a child. They are the bridge to the outside world of resources that sustain life. In both giving and receiving resources, boundaries play an important role. In the beginning, parents are the source. They progressively give children the independence to obtain what they need on their own.

- Boundaries facilitate the process of having the child internalize things—feeling the need or motivation to take responsibility for himself, planning for and taking the time to act responsibly, developing the skills necessary to act responsibly—that were once external to him.

- When parents take a stance of clear boundaries with a child, the child will have a better chance of gaining the motivation, the need, the skill, and the plan to live a loving, responsible, righteous, and successful life unto God and others. This is what character is all about.

you are watching. You can use these later to review what was covered. Now, let's take a look at our first video.

> View Video Segment: Parenting with an Eye to the Future.

10 minutes ### Kid Talk: What's a Mom to Do?

> Participant's Guide pages 15–16.

Let's discuss the situation we have just seen. Please turn to page 15 of your Participant's Guide.

1. Why didn't Cameron feel the need to clean up his room? What kept him from being motivated to clean up?

> Possible answers: Allison loved "helping" Cameron, and he had developed a pattern in which he felt entitled to everyone else's help.

2. Why didn't Cameron plan for or take the time to clean up? Why didn't he have the skill to organize his room?

> Possible answers: Cameron had never needed to plan for or take time to clean up. Allison had always helped him, and, consequently, he hadn't developed the necessary skills either.

3. In what other areas of life can parents inadvertently keep kids from taking responsibility for themselves? As you consider these specific examples, think about how you—like Allison—may be keeping your child from taking responsibility for himself.

> Possible answers: Homework, household chores, or meeting school deadlines.

4. What kind of boundaries could Allison establish for herself in order for her son to develop boundaries that would serve him well?

> Possible answers: Allison could give Cameron time limits for learning to take care of his belongings, outline what would happen if he did not learn, and stick to those consequences.

5. In what ways might you, like Allison, be parenting in the present without thinking about the future?

PLANNING NOTES

_____

_____

_____

_____

_____

_____

_____

_____

_____

_____

_____

_____

_____

_____

_____

_____

_____

_____

_____

_____

_____

KID TALK
What's a Mom to Do?

1. Why didn't Cameron feel the need to clean up his room? What kept him from being motivated to clean up?

2. Why didn't Cameron plan for or take the time to clean up? Why didn't he have the skill to organize his room?

3. Where, if at all, are you—like Allison—keeping your child from taking responsibility for himself?

4. What kind of boundaries could Allison establish for herself in order for her son to develop boundaries that would serve him well?

5. In what ways might you, like Allison, be parenting in the present without thinking about the future?

---

6. What can we, as parents, do to keep an eye on the future?

7. What possible courses of action could Allison take that would indicate that she has an eye on the future?

> Possible answers: Making excuses for your kids when they fail; covering for them when they miss a school deadline; lying for them.

6. What can we, as parents, do to keep an eye on the future?

> Possible answers: Pray and ask God to give us an awareness of how our actions today could be shaping tomorrow. Talk to parents of older kids to learn from their successes as well as their mistakes.

7. What possible courses of action could Allison take which would indicate that she has an eye on the future?

> Possible answers: Continue the program of boundaries and consequences for Cameron. Learn from other parents what they've done to raise responsible kids. Look at other aspects of her parenting to see where she is standing in the way of Cameron's independence.

With Allison's example in our mind, let's now look at our own parenting and consider how well we're fulfilling the key roles of guardian, manager, and source.

10 minutes   *Kid Kare: The Parent as Guardian, Manager, and Source*

> Participant's Guide pages 17–18.

Please turn to page 17, where you will find the exercise The Parent as Guardian, Manager, and Source.

Directions

We will be doing this exercise in small groups of three or four people. Answer the questions within your group, giving each person an opportunity to share. You'll have 10 minutes to complete this exercise. Any questions?

> Let the participants know when there is 1 minute remaining. Call the group back together after 10 minutes.

Who would like to share an experience from their group?

> Solicit answers from the groups.

That's great! Now that we've had a chance to think about parenting with an eye on the future, let's take a look at the kind of character we want to develop in our children for that future.

PLANNING NOTES

_____

_____

_____

_____

_____

_____

_____

_____

_____

_____

_____

_____

_____

---

6. What can we, as parents, do to keep an eye on the future?

7. What possible courses of action could Allison take that would indicate that she has an eye on the future?

KID KARE

The Parent as Guardian, Manager, and Source

DIRECTIONS

In small groups of three or four people, answer the questions below, giving each person an opportunity to share. You will have 10 minutes to complete this exercise.

GUARDIAN

1. A guardian is legally responsible for a child and, in that capacity, protects and preserves the child. Balancing freedom and limits becomes a major task in child rearing. Which of the following sources of danger is one of your children facing? Give an example of a boundary or limit you could set to protect your child. Who will help you stand strong as your child tests that limit?

    - Dangers within themselves
    - Dangers in the outside world
    - Inappropriate freedoms they are not ready to handle
    - Inappropriate or evil actions, behaviors, or attitudes
    - Their own regressive tendency to remain dependent and avoid growing up

MANAGER

2. A manager makes sure things get done—that goals are reached, demands and expectations are met. Children are not born with self-discipline; therefore they have to have "other-discipline." Managers provide this other-discipline for a child's needs by controlling resources, teaching, enforcing consequences, correcting, chastising, maintaining order, and building life skills. With which of the following situations are you currently dealing? What could a boundary-wise parent do? Be specific.

- Finishing chores
- Getting homework done
- Learning to be kind and loving
- Being honest
- Using talents
- Other

SOURCE

3. Parents are the source of all good things (material and immaterial) for a child. They are the bridge to the outside world of resources that sustain life. In both giving and receiving resources, boundaries play an important role. Think of a common scenario in your family where you tend to give too easily or to hold resources too tightly. What risk do you run with that tendency? At this point, what do you think you could do to counter that tendency?

6 minutes   ## *Video Segment: Eight Key Aspects of Character*

> Remind the participants that key points of the video segment can be found on pages 19–21 of the Participant's Guide if they would like to review them at a later time.

> View Video Segment: Eight Key Aspects of Character.

8 minutes   ## *Kid Kare: Cultivating Character*

> Participant's Guide pages 22–23.

As we just discovered, character building is indeed a tall order! The exercise on pages 22–23 of your Participant's Guide attempts to break this process down into more manageable pieces.

Directions

On your own or with your spouse, you will have 10 minutes to begin working through the following questions. You will have a chance to complete this exercise and put it into action at home this week. Any questions?

> Let the participants know when there is 1 minute remaining. Call the group back together after 10 minutes.

1 MINUTE   WRAP-UP

> Participant's Guide pages 24–25.

Before we close in prayer, please turn to pages 24–25 of your Participant's Guide. Each of our *Boundaries with Kids* sessions ends with a section called Kid Kare at Home. This section will provide you with an opportunity to put into action some of the ideas you've had as you've watched the videos and talked with others in the class. We'll take a few minutes at the beginning of each session to follow up on what some of you did at home so that we can learn from each other. Now let's close in prayer.

Closing Prayer

Almighty God, you call us to parent with an eye to the future and to serve as a guardian, manager, and source for our kids. You've cho-

PLANNING NOTES

_____

_____

_____

_____

_____

_____

_____

_____

_____

_____

_____

_____

_____

_____

VIDEO SEGMENT
Eight Key Aspects of Character

Dr. Cloud and Dr. Townsend outline eight qualities they consider important to adult functioning. In each of these qualities, boundaries play an essential developmental role:

- **Loving**—Most parents would say that they want their children to be loving. Loving people recognize that the world does not revolve around them. They are able to control their impulses, respect the boundaries of others, and set boundaries for themselves so that they are responsible people whose actions are loving.

- **Responsible**—Being responsible means taking ownership of your life. Ownership is to truly possess your life and to know that you are accountable for it—to God and others. Responsibility therefore includes such things as duty or obligations, reliability and dependability, and just "getting the job done." Responsible people also take ownership of their feelings, attitudes, behaviors, choices, limits, talents, thoughts, desires, values, and loves—things our boundaries define and protect.

- **Free**—People with healthy character are free people. In sharp contrast to today's popular victim mentality, free people realize that they can act rather than remain passive in a situation, that they have choices and can take some control of their life. Children raised with good boundaries learn they are not only responsible for their lives but are also free to live their lives any way they choose—as long as they take responsibility for their choices.

- **Initiating**—A normal part of human behavior is to initiate things. Being created in the image of God is

---

being created with the ability to begin something. Teaching a child to initiate is an important aspect of boundary training.

- **Respectful of Reality**—In order for someone to create a life that works he or she must have a healthy respect for reality. By reality we mean experiencing the consequences of our actions in the real world. Mature adults know that, for the most part, if they do good, good things will happen; if they do nothing or do something bad, bad things will happen. This dual respect for the positive and negative sides of reality is often referred to as wisdom.

- **Oriented to Growth**—Good parenting can help a child develop character that faces the obstacles of life with an orientation toward growth. This includes developing abilities and gaining knowledge as well as facing negative things about oneself that invite growth and change. Boundaries help children see what is expected of them and how they might grow to meet those expectations. Parents should require their children to do the changing instead of trying to get reality to change.

- **Oriented to Truth**—Honesty begins with parents who model it, require it from their children, and provide them with a safe environment in which to be honest. Boundaries provide the safety of known consequences for failure. Children can handle the known logical consequences of their mistakes much better than they can handle relational consequences like anger, guilt, shame, condemnation, or abandonment.

- **Oriented to Transcendence**—The most important questions anyone can answer are "Who is God?" and "Is it me, or is it God?" Being grounded in God gives direction and meaning to human existence, allowing

---

us to transcend life, problems, our own limitations and mistakes, and other people's sins against us. People who have the ability to transcend themselves go beyond their own existence to the reality of others, of God, and of virtues they hold more important than themselves and their own immediate happiness.

- A child's character will determine much of the course his life takes. To develop a child of good character, we must be parents of good character.

KID KARE
Cultivating Character

DIRECTIONS

Take 10 minutes to complete this exercise on your own or with your spouse. You will have a chance to complete this exercise and put it into action at home this week.

LOVING

What are you doing or could you be doing to teach your children to be more loving and to be more respectful of people's boundaries?

RESPONSIBLE

When have you recently seen your child hesitate or even fail to take responsibility for her feelings, attitudes, behaviors, choices, limits, talents, thoughts, desires, values, or loves? Why did she hesitate? What was your response—and what do you want your response to be next time?

FREE

Where, if at all, are you letting your child claim to be a victim rather than encouraging him to be responsible for what is happening in his life? Consider, for instance, his friendships, school situations, and involvement in sports.

INITIATING

What are you doing (or could you be doing) to teach your child that he is responsible for his own fun, goals, and happiness and that he must actively pursue them?

RESPECTFUL OF REALITY

What are you doing or could you be doing to teach your child that accomplishment comes one day at a time, and that goofing off and laziness will cost her?

GROWING

Being able to grow includes the ability to

- Recover from distressing emotional states
- Sustain periods of negative strain and delay gratification
- Lose well, grieve, and let go of what cannot be reclaimed or won
- Confess when you are wrong
- Change behavior or direction when confronted with reality
- Forgive
- Take ownership of a problem

Which of these abilities does your child need to work on? What will you do to help her?

ORIENTED TO TRUTH

What are you teaching your child about honesty through your words? Your actions? What logical consequences have you established or would you like to establish for those times when your child is less than honest?

ORIENTED TO TRANSCENDENCE

Without an orientation to transcend the realities of this life and touch the realities of God, people are very limited. What are you saying and doing to orient your child to transcendence? What step will you take this week?

Closing Prayer

Almighty God, you call me to parent with an eye to the future and to serve as a guardian, manager, and source for my kids. You've chosen me to help my children become people who are loving, responsible, free, initiating, respectful of reality, growing, oriented to truth, and oriented to transcendence. I've heard that if I have good, clear boundaries with my children, they will have a better chance of gaining the motivation, the need, the skill, and the plan to live a loving, responsible, righteous, and successful life unto you and others. In light of such a tall order, it is good to remind myself that when you call someone to serve, you also empower that person. May I know your power in my parenting this week—the power of your wisdom, your patience, your creativity, and your love. Here I am, Lord, humbled by this daunting responsibility and ready to be used by you. I pray in Jesus' name. Amen.

Kid Kare at Home

1. Look back at Cultivating Character on page 22. Finish the exercise if you haven't already done so. Now choose one quality to work on with your child this week.

2. Things we want to teach our kids—and even some things we don't want them to learn!—are often "more caught than taught." None of us can be entirely sure what our kids are "catching" from us. Spend some

---

time this week asking God to show you where you could be learning to be more loving, responsible, free, initiating, respectful of reality, growing, oriented to truth, and oriented to transcendence. His answer will probably move you out of your comfort zone, but know that it is an opportunity for your own growth.

3. This week, catch your kid doing something right! Celebrate with a high five or a big bear hug!

BETWEEN SESSIONS READING

"The Future Is Now" and "What Does Character Look Like?" chapters 1 and 2 in *Boundaries with Kids*.

sen us to help our children become people who are loving, responsible, free, initiating, respectful of reality, growing, oriented to truth, and oriented to transcendence. We've heard that if we have good, clear boundaries with our children, they will have a better chance of gaining the motivation, the need, the skill, and the plan to live a loving, responsible, righteous, and successful life unto you and others. In light of such a tall order, it is good to remind ourselves that when you call someone to serve, you also empower that person. May we know your power in our parenting this week—the power of your wisdom, your patience, your creativity, and your love. Here we are, Lord, humbled by this daunting responsibility and ready to be used by you. We pray in Jesus' name. Amen.

Have a great week! Blessings on your Kid Kare at Home efforts— and don't forget to enjoy your kids!

PLANNING NOTES

_____

_____

_____

_____

_____

_____

_____

_____

_____

_____

_____

_____

_____

_____

_____

_____

_____

_____

_____

_____

_____

_____

_____

_____

Closing Prayer

Almighty God, you call me to parent with an eye to the future and to serve as a guardian, manager, and source for my kids. You've chosen me to help my children become people who are loving, responsible, free, initiating, respectful of reality, growing, oriented to truth, and oriented to transcendence. I've heard that if I have good, clear boundaries with my children, they will have a better chance of gaining the motivation, the need, the skill, and the plan to live a loving, responsible, righteous, and successful life unto you and others. In light of such a tall order, it is good to remind myself that when you call someone to serve, you also empower that person. May I know your power in my parenting this week—the power of your wisdom, your patience, your creativity, and your love. Here I am, Lord, humbled by this daunting responsibility and ready to be used by you. I pray in Jesus' name. Amen.

Kid Kare at Home

1. Look back at Cultivating Character on page 22. Finish the exercise if you haven't already done so. Now choose one quality to work on with your child this week.

2. Things we want to teach our kids—and even some things we don't want them to learn!—are often "more caught than taught." None of us can be entirely sure what our kids are "catching" from us. Spend some

---

time this week asking God to show you where you could be learning to be more loving, responsible, free, initiating, respectful of reality, growing, oriented to truth, and oriented to transcendence. His answer will probably move you out of your comfort zone, but know that it is an opportunity for your own growth.

3. This week, catch your kid doing something right! Celebrate with a high five or a big bear hug!

BETWEEN SESSIONS READING

"The Future Is Now" and "What Does Character Look Like?" chapters 1 and 2 in *Boundaries with Kids*.

Session Two

Kids Need Parents with Boundaries

BEFORE YOU LEAD

Key Points

- "Problem kids" don't evolve in a vacuum. Problem children generally have a problem context.

- Who we are today is essentially the result of two forces: our environment and our responses to it.

- We parents need to interpret our child's behavior both as a response to our own behavior as well as in terms of her motives, needs, personality, and circumstances.

- Basically, children will mature to the level at which the parent structures them, and not higher.

- Parents can influence their kids to develop boundaries in three ways: by teaching, by modeling, and by helping them internalize healthy boundaries.

- Teaching boundaries is difficult. Part of the challenge is tolerating and enduring your child's hatred of your boundaries. The kid's job is to test her parents' resolve, so she can learn about reality. The parent's job is to withstand that test, including the child's anger, pouting, tantrums, and much more.

Synopsis

Problem kids don't evolve in a vacuum. Problem children generally have a problem context. In the same way, kids with healthy boundaries don't grow their boundaries out of thin air. While our very nature causes us to resist limits, we have a lot of help with either developing boundaries or not developing them.

As Christians and psychologists, Dr. Cloud and Dr. Townsend live in two different environments. The religious world sometimes blames problems on the child, saying it's all "in Suzie's sinful nature." The counseling world sometimes blames the parents, placing all out-of-control behaviors on "what happened to Suzie as a child." Neither of these views is completely accurate. Who we are today is essentially the

31

result of two forces: our environment and our responses to it. Our parenting, significant relationships, and circumstances powerfully shape our character and attitudes. But how we react to our significant relationships and circumstances—whether defensively or responsibly—also influences what kind of person we become.

In light of this fact, we parents need to interpret our child's behavior both as a response to our own behavior and in terms of her motives, needs, personality, and circumstances. As a rule, children don't know what they are doing. They have little idea how to handle life so that it works right. That's why God gave them parents—to love them, give them structure, and guide them into maturity. Basically, children will mature to the level at which the parent structures them, and not higher.

Looking at the plank in their own eye rather than the speck of sawdust in their child's (see Matthew 7:1–5) may be painful for parents, but doing so will help them recognize the work they could do on themselves. Repairing and developing boundaries with God and with other growing people will help parents develop a child with boundaries. In addition, parents can influence their kids to develop boundaries in three ways: by teaching, by modeling, and by helping them internalize healthy boundaries.

Clearly, teaching boundaries is difficult. Part of the challenge is tolerating and enduring a child's natural hatred of boundaries. The kid's job is to test a parent's resolve, so she can learn about reality. The parent's job is to withstand that test, including the child's anger, pouting, tantrums, and much more. No wonder most parents struggle to maintain boundaries and to train their children to develop them!

Further complicating a parent's boundary-training efforts are certain obstacles:

1. **Depending on the child.** If you are afraid that if you say no to your kids, you will lose the love you need from them, consider where you are getting the love you need (Genesis 2:18) or where you could be getting it.

2. **Overidentifying with the child.** If you find that you can't bear your child's pain, you may be projecting your pain onto him. Consider first what past issues that have not fully healed may be causing you to overidentify with your child—and then what you will do to resolve those issues.

3. **Thinking love and separateness are enemies.** Disagreeing, confronting, or simply being different from your children does not indicate a break in the connection. Structuring and being separate from your child are not the same thing as a loss of love.

4. **Ignoring and "zapping."** Both ignoring and zapping teach the child he should persist in whatever he wants. He learns he can get away with murder nine times out of ten, and he just needs to learn how to endure the out-of-control parent that one time out of ten.

5. **Being worn down.** Kids work us and work us and work us. It is scary how they can sense when we are weak and ready to give in to them! Take a moment to consider why your child may be wearing you down. And remember that kids with parents who pursue their own interests rather than solely focus on their kids learn both that they aren't the center of the universe and that they can be free to pursue their own dreams.

When it comes to training kids in boundaries, parents do well to realize that they can't teach what they don't have. Parents can't just *say* boundaries to their child; they must *be* boundaries.

Session Outline (48 minutes)

    I. Introduction (10 minutes)
      A. Welcome (1 minute)
      B. Review and Overview (8 minutes)
      C. Opening Prayer (1 minute)
   II. Discovery (36 minutes)
      A. Video Segment: Boundaries for Kids—and Their Parents (5 minutes)
      B. Kid Talk: Three Avenues of Influence (8 minutes)
      C. Video Segment: Overcoming Obstacles to Boundary Training (5 minutes)
      D. Kid Talk: Five Obstacles to Boundary Training (10 minutes)
      E. Kid Kare: Withstanding Your Kid's Testing (8 minutes)
  III. Wrap-up (2 minutes)

Recommended Reading

"Kids Need Parents with Boundaries," chapter 3 in *Boundaries with Kids.*

Session Two

Kids Need Parents with Boundaries

10 MINUTES INTRODUCTION

1 minute · Welcome

> Call the group together and welcome the participants to Session 2: Kids Need Parents with Boundaries.

8 minutes · Review and Overview

> Participant's Guide page 27.

It's good to be with all of you again, and I know it will be good and encouraging to hear how your week has gone. You had several different kinds of Kid Kare to try this week, and I trust some of you are willing to share some details from the home front.

We'll start with a few easy questions. Who caught a child doing something right? What effect did your noticing that act have on your child? On your relationship with your child?

> Note: Be ready to share an anecdote from your own life.

Last week we talked about eight important character qualities. You can look on pages 22 and 23 of your Participant's Guide for the list. We want our children to be loving, responsible, free, initiating, respectful of reality, growing, oriented to truth, and oriented to transcendence. Who, since we last met, did something to help your child grow in one of these areas? What did you do? What was your child's response?

> Note: Again, be ready to share an anecdote from your own life.

PLANNING NOTES

_____

_____

_____

_____

_____

_____

_____

_____

_____

_____

_____

_____

_____

_____

Session Two

Kids Need Parents with Boundaries

OVERVIEW

In this session, you will

• Consider how your kids' behavior is a response to their environment, of which parents are a big part.

• Think about the fact that boundaries are more caught than taught—and begin to see which of your boundaries are contagious.

• Look at three ways that parents can influence their kids to develop boundaries: by teaching, by modeling, and by helping kids internalize healthy boundaries.

• Acknowledge that part of the challenge of teaching kids boundaries is tolerating and enduring your child's hatred of your boundaries. The kid's job is to test your resolve, so she can learn about reality. Your job is to withstand that test, including your child's anger, pouting, tantrums, and much more.

• Recognize five obstacles to teaching kids boundaries: depending on the child, overidentifying with the child, thinking that love and separateness are enemies, ignoring and zapping, and being worn down.

27

KID KARE

Cultivating Character

DIRECTIONS

Take 10 minutes to complete this exercise on your own or with your spouse. You will have a chance to complete this exercise and put it into action at home this week.

LOVING

What are you doing or could you be doing to teach your children to be more loving and to be more respectful of people's boundaries?

RESPONSIBLE

When have you recently seen your child hesitate or even fail to take responsibility for her feelings, attitudes, behaviors, choices, limits, talents, thoughts, desires, values, or loves? Why did she hesitate? What was your response—and what do you want your response to be next time?

FREE

Where, if at all, are you letting your child claim to be a victim rather than encouraging him to be responsible for what is happening in his life? Consider, for instance, his friendships, school situations, and involvement in sports.

INITIATING

What are you doing (or could you be doing) to teach your child that he is responsible for his own fun, goals, and happiness and that he must actively pursue them?

RESPECTFUL OF REALITY

What are you doing or could you be doing to teach your child that accomplishment comes one day at a time, and that goofing off and laziness will cost her?

GROWING

Being able to grow includes the ability to
• Recover from distressing emotional states
• Sustain periods of negative strain and delay gratification
• Lose well, grieve, and let go of what cannot be reclaimed or won
• Confess when you are wrong
• Change behavior or direction when confronted with reality
• Forgive
• Take ownership of a problem

Which of these abilities does your child need to work on? What will you do to help her?

ORIENTED TO TRUTH

What are you teaching your child about honesty through your words? Your actions? What logical consequences have you established or would you like to establish for those times when your child is less than honest?

ORIENTED TO TRANSCENDENCE

Without an orientation to transcend the realities of this life and touch the realities of God, people are very limited. What are you saying and doing to orient your child to transcendence? What step will you take this week?

Thanks for sharing your experiences. Just because we're moving on doesn't mean we should stop thinking about these eight aspects of character. It is wise to take a long-term view of the kind of character we want to be building into our children as we learn about how boundaries can help us succeed in that important undertaking.

As Dr. Townsend said last week, to develop a child of good character we have to be parents of good character. Since healthy boundaries contribute to good character, it follows that kids need parents with healthy boundaries.

In today's session, we will consider which of our boundaries are contagious and how to teach boundaries to our kids by instructing, modeling, and helping kids internalize healthy boundaries. We'll see that we need to be able to both endure our kids' hatred of boundaries and overcome five obstacles to teaching them boundaries: depending on the child, overidentifying with the child, thinking that love and separateness are enemies, ignoring and zapping, and being worn down.

Let's open with a word of prayer.

1 minute   *Opening Prayer*

Lord God, thank you for the difference in our parenting that some here are already sensing after only one week. We thank you that nothing is impossible with you—no situation with our kids, no habit that seems entrenched, no character weakness that seems ingrained. Today we're looking at ourselves and our boundaries. Holy Spirit, please soften our hearts, remove our defenses, and grow us to be people with healthier boundaries, people of good character whose lives will glorify God. We pray in Jesus' name. Amen.

36 MINUTES DISCOVERY

5 minutes   *Video Segment: Boundaries for Kids—and Their Parents*

You may have been hoping that this series would focus on your kids, but in order to understand our kids we do well to look both at the context for growing up that we parents give them and at what we are modeling, however consciously or unconsciously. When it comes to the issue of boundaries, that means taking a good look at ourselves. Dr. Cloud and Dr. Townsend will begin addressing this point in today's first video segment, Boundaries for Kids—and Their Parents.

> Remind the participants that key points of the video segment can be found on pages 28 and 29 of the Participant's Guide if they would like to review them at a later time.

PLANNING NOTES

_____

_____

_____

_____

_____

_____

_____

_____

_____

_____

_____

_____

_____

_____

_____

_____

_____

_____

_____

_____

_____

VIDEO SEGMENT
Boundaries for Kids—and Their Parents

- "Problem kids" don't evolve in a vacuum. Problem children generally have a problem context, and kids with healthy boundaries don't grow them out of thin air.

- As Christians and psychologists, Dr. Cloud and Dr. Townsend live in two different environments. The religious world sometimes blames problems on the child, saying it's all "in Suzie's sinful nature." The counseling world sometimes blames the parents, placing all out-of-control behaviors on "what happened to Suzie as a child." Neither of these views is completely accurate.

- Who we are today is essentially the result of two forces: our environment and our responses to it. Our parenting, significant relationships, and circumstances powerfully shape our character and attitudes. But how we react to our significant relationships and circumstances—whether defensively or responsibly—also influences what kind of person we become.

- In light of this fact, we parents need to interpret our child's behavior both as a response to our own behavior as well as in terms of her motives, needs, personality, and circumstances.

- Basically, children will mature to the level at which the parent structures them, and not higher. Looking at the plank in your eye rather than the speck of sawdust in your child's (see Matthew 7:1–5) may be painful, but it will help you recognize the work you could do on yourself.

- Parents can influence their kids to develop boundaries in three ways. First, you can teach your children boundaries—the ability to hear and say no appropriately—just as you teach them to tie their shoes, ride a bike, or clean their rooms.

- Second, you can model boundaries. Children learn about boundaries from how you operate in your own world. They watch how you treat them, your spouse, and your work—and they emulate you, for good or for bad. In this sense, boundaries are "caught" more than they are "taught."

- Third, you can help your child internalize healthy boundaries. To internalize something is to make it part of yourself. If you "do" boundaries with your kids, they internalize the experiences, remember them, digest them, and make them part of how they see reality.

- Teaching boundaries is difficult! Part of the challenge is tolerating and enduring your child's hatred of your boundaries. The kid's job is to test your resolve, so she can learn about reality. Your job is to withstand that test, including your child's anger, pouting, tantrums, and much more.

> View Video Segment: Boundaries for Kids — and Their Parents.

8 minutes

Kid Kare: Three Avenues of Influence

> Participant's Guide pages 30–31.

In the video just now, Dr. Cloud and Dr. Townsend outlined three ways we can influence our kids to develop boundaries—through teaching, modeling, and internalizing. Please turn to pages 30 and 31 of your Participant's Guide.

Directions

For this exercise, we will break into three groups. I will assign each group one of the three avenues of influence discussed in the video segment. Discuss the topic your group has been assigned, making sure everyone has a chance to participate. You will have 8 minutes to complete this exercise. Any questions?

> Let the participants know when there is 1 minute remaining. Call the group back together after 8 minutes.

5 minutes

Video Segment: Overcoming Obstacles to Boundary Training

As Dr. Townsend said in the video, teaching boundaries is difficult. In this next video, we are going to look at some obstacles that contribute to that difficulty in hopes of making this important parenting task a bit easier.

> Remind the participants that key points of the video segment can be found on pages 32–34 of the Participant's Guide if they would like to review them at a later time.

> View Video Segment: Overcoming Obstacles to Boundary Training.

10 minutes

Kid Talk: Five Obstacles to Boundary Training

> Participant's Guide pages 35–36.

Let's talk a bit more about these five obstacles to boundary training. Please turn to pages 35 and 36 of your Participant's Guide.

PLANNING NOTES

_____

_____

_____

_____

_____

_____

_____

_____

_____

_____

_____

_____

_____

_____

_____

_____

_____

_____

KID KARE
Three Avenues of Influence

DIRECTIONS

Take the next 5 minutes in your group and discuss one of the three avenues of influence discussed in the video segment, making sure everyone has a chance to participate.

TEACHING

1. Like teaching a child to tie their shoes, ride a bike, or clean their rooms, you can directly teach your kids boundaries—the ability to hear and say no appropriately. What could a parent say to a child, using the word boundary or a boundary principle, in each of the following situations? You can find suggested responses on page 41.

   • Jill defiantly refuses to stop screaming in anger at you.

   • Sophie continually fails to display proper table manners.

   • Nate says that he'd get better grades if he had a computer in his bedroom, if he weren't sitting at the same table as Aaron, and if he didn't have to do chores at home.

   • Aaron is consistently late for dinner with the family.

   • Elizabeth is having trouble being nice to her preschool friend. She will grab toys and even hit Katherine when she gets frustrated.

2. What recent situation could have been an opportunity for you to use the word *boundary* with your kids? Why would doing so have been helpful?

MODELING

1. Boundaries are caught more than they are taught. In which of the following areas could your efforts to live out healthy boundaries in your own life be more consistent with what you are trying to teach your child about boundaries? You can find suggested responses on page 42.

   • Everyday conversation

   • Healthy eating

   • Helping around the house

   • Busyness and the value of rest

   • Priorities

   • Other

2. What step will you take this week to strengthen your boundaries in one of the areas you just identified?

HELPING YOUR CHILD INTERNALIZE

1. If your boundary training consists only of words, you are wasting your breath. But if you "do" boundaries with your kids, they will internalize the experiences. In order for a child to develop boundaries, a parent with boundaries must stand like an oak tree that a child runs her head into over and over again until she realizes that the tree is stronger than she is and she walks around it next time. In what areas of parenting are you standing strong like an oak? What lessons is that helping your children learn?

2. In what areas could you strengthen your boundaries so you can stand stronger?

VIDEO SEGMENT
Overcoming Obstacles to Boundary Training

• "If you can't stand the heat, stay out of the kitchen" goes the old saying. Part of the heat of parenting is tolerating and enduring your child's hatred of your boundaries. A child's job is to test your resolve, so she can learn about reality. Your job is to withstand the test, including your child's anger, pouting, tantrums, and much more.

• Teaching boundaries is difficult, but being aware of five obstacles when teaching boundaries may help that challenging course be a little less difficult!

1. **Depending on the child.** As your child's major source of love, you provide the closeness, intimacy, and nurture that sustains her. Yet this closeness can become confused with a parent's need for the child. This is called dependency. It is the reverse of what the parenting relationship should be. If you are afraid that if you say no to your kids, you will lose the love you need from them, consider where you are getting the love you need (Genesis 2:18) or where you could be getting it.

2. **Overidentifying with the child.** Children need their parents to empathize with their pain, fear, and loneliness. But some parents confuse their own painful feelings with their child's and project their problems onto the child. What might be discomfort for a toddler is seen as trauma by the mother. If you find that you can't bear your child's pain, you may be projecting your pain onto him. Consider any past issues that have not fully healed that may be causing you to overidentify with your child—and what you will do to resolve those issues.

---

3. **Thinking love and separateness are enemies.** Disagreeing, confronting, or simply being different from your children does not indicate a break in the connection. Structuring and being separate from your child are not the same thing as a loss of love. If you feel that when you tell the truth to your child, love is gone, then begin working on being a truthful, honest person with God and the supportive people in your life.

4. **Ignoring and zapping.** Ignoring and zapping teaches a child that he can persist in doing whatever he wants. By ignoring inappropriate behavior and not addressing things as they happen, he learns he can get away with murder nine times out of ten. When a parent finally reaches his saturation point, he lashes out in rage (thus, "zapping" a child) over a situation he had previously ignored. When the child is zapped he internalizes an attacking voice instead of reality limits. Angry voices become internal critics, or worse, the child either buckles under with guilt and depression or ignores his parents until he gets a zapping of his own making.

5. **Being worn down.** Kids work us and work us and work us. It is scary how they can sense when we are weak and ready to give in to them. Take a moment to consider why your child may be wearing you down. And remember that kids with parents who pursue their own interests rather than solely focus on their kids learn both that they aren't the center of the universe and that they can be free to pursue their own dreams.

• When it comes to training your kids in boundaries, remember that you can't teach what you don't have.

Don't just *say* boundaries to your child; *be* boundaries. If you aren't yet, get to work on yourself. It will pay off for both you and your child.

1. The first obstacle discussed was that of depending on the child. Why is it a problem for the parent as well as the child when a parent needs a child's closeness or affection to meet their own unmet needs?

> Possible answers: Parents keep turning to their kids to meet their unmet needs for closeness or affection. A parent's dependency on a child can compromise the parent's ability to structure appropriate limits with the child—and parenting doesn't get any easier when that happens.

2. The second obstacle was overidentifying with the child. What is the difference between *hurt* and *harm?* Why is this distinction important in parenting?

> Possible answers: Harm does change whereas hurt is more superficial. We need to let our kids know the hurt of disappointment, of not getting their own way, of failing, etc. These hurts teach and strengthen kids rather than harm them.

3. The third obstacle stated was thinking of love and separateness as enemies. Explain the statement, "You can't really love someone with whom you can't be separate. That is, love does not mean losing yourself, but rather frees you and empowers you to be yourself." What bearing does this statement have on parenting?

> Possible answers: We need to provide our kids with freedom—and limits to that freedom—so they can become healthy independent of us. We need to let our kids be who God created and calls them to be, not images of ourselves or puppets living out our unrealized dreams. Such freedom gives parents and children the opportunity to truly love each other.

4. The fourth obstacle to boundary training was that of ignoring and "zapping." Why is ignoring an unhelpful approach to a child's inappropriate behavior? What harm can zapping cause? Why is consistency in confronting problem behaviors early in the game important preparation for real life?

> Possible answers: Ignoring inappropriate behavior wrongly suggests that it is acceptable. Zapping is harmful because a parent's inconsistency can be experienced as a lack of trustworthiness (will she react this time?), and it may also suggest moral relativism (sometimes this is bad; sometimes it isn't). Consistency early on is crucial because children don't have internal brakes on their inappropriate behavior, so they need their parents to be their external boundary.

PLANNING NOTES

_____

_____

_____

_____

_____

_____

_____

_____

_____

_____

_____

_____

_____

_____

_____

_____

_____

_____

_____

Session Two: *Kids Need Parents with Boundaries*   35

KID TALK

Five Obstacles to Boundary Training

1. The first obstacle discussed was that of depending on the child. Why is it a problem for the parent as well as the child when a parent needs a child's closeness or affection to meet their own unmet needs?

2. The second obstacle was overidentifying with the child. What is the difference between *hurt* and *harm?* Why is this distinction important in parenting?

3. The third obstacle stated was that of thinking love and separateness are enemies. Explain the statement, "You can't really love someone with whom you can't be separate. That is, love does not mean losing yourself but rather frees you and empowers you to be yourself." What bearing does this statement have on parenting?

4. The fourth obstacle to boundary training was that of ignoring and "zapping." Why is ignoring an unhelpful approach to a child's inappropriate behavior? What harm can zapping cause? Why is consistency in confronting problem behaviors early in the game important preparation for real life?

---

36   *Boundaries with Kids Participant's Guide*

5. The final boundary discussed was that of being worn down. What can parents teach their kids from the relationships they maintain and the things they do to fill up their tank?

5. The final boundary discussed was that of being worn down. What can parents teach their kids from the relationships they maintain and the things they do to fill up their tank?

> Possible answers: Parents who pursue their own interests, relationships, and activities teach their kids that they aren't the center of the universe. These parents are also modeling the freedom to pursue their own dreams.

Now that we've discussed five obstacles to teaching boundaries, let's look at what you can do to take care of yourself so you can take better care of your kids.

8 minutes

Growing As a Parent: Withstanding Your Kid's Testing

> Participant's Guide pages 37–39.

Directions

The questions on pages 37 through 39 are designed to help you be able to stand strong when your child tests you on each of the five fronts we've been discussing. On your own, spend the next 8 minutes working through them.

> Let the participants know when there is 1 minute remaining. Call the group back together after 8 minutes.

2 MINUTES   WRAP-UP

> Participant's Guide pages 40–43.

I'd encourage you to take time this week to finish any exercise you started but didn't have time to complete. Also, under Kid Kare at Home on pages 40 through 43 you'll find a few other things to think about and act on this week. Now let's close in prayer.

Closing Prayer

Lord God, we know all too well the natural tendency to fight against boundaries. We do that with you all the time, so it should come as no surprise that our kids fight boundaries as well. Guide us as we teach and model boundaries. Give us strength when our children test those boundaries, and grant us patience and compassion when they are

PLANNING NOTES

_____

_____

_____

_____

_____

_____

_____

_____

_____

_____

_____

_____

_____

_____

_____

_____

_____

_____

_____

---

5. The final boundary discussed was that of being worn down. What can parents teach their kids from the relationships they maintain and the things they do to fill up their tank?

KID KARE

Withstanding Your Kid's Testing

DIRECTIONS

Taking care of yourself can help you take better care of your kids. The following questions are designed to help you stand strong when your child tests you on each of the five fronts we've been discussing. On your own, spend the next 8 minutes working through them.

DEPENDING ON THE CHILD

1. Are you afraid that if you say no to your kids, you will lose the love you need from them? To help you answer that tough question, consider where you are getting the love you need (Genesis 2:18) or where you could be getting it.

2. In what areas are you not setting limits because you fear losing your child's love? What will you do differently now that you have recognized this dynamic? Whom will you call to help you and hold you accountable for setting clear and firm boundaries for your children?

OVERIDENTIFYING WITH THE CHILD

1. If you find that you can't bear your child's pain, you may be projecting your pain into him. What past issues that have not fully healed may be causing you to overidentify with your child? What will you do to resolve those issues? Who will help you?

---

2. When did you recently fail in discipline because you overidentified with your child's pain? What was the situation? What were you feeling? What current issues are you overidentifying with and, as a result, not disciplining?

THINKING LOVE AND SEPARATENESS ARE ENEMIES

1. If you feel that love is gone when you tell the truth to your child, begin working on being a truthful, honest person with God and the supportive people in your life. What keeps you from being honest? Share those fears honestly with God. With whom can you practice being open and truthful?

2. In the past week or so, when did you choose not to confront, disagree with, or simply be different from your child because you were more concerned about him feeling loved? What ongoing issue(s) about which you've been silent would you be wise to address honestly and as soon as possible?

IGNORING AND ZAPPING

1. Do you see a pattern of ignoring and zapping in your parenting? Have you been labeling it "patience"? Who can help you grow in the area of confrontation, of speaking the truth in love?

---

2. What aspect of your child's behavior have you been ignoring but resenting, moving closer to the boiling point? Put another way, what aspect of your child's behavior would you be wise to confront even if it's not especially early in the game? What will you say when you do confront him?

BEING WORN DOWN

1. Parenting is a temporary (albeit sometimes consuming) job, not an identity. Who are you apart from a parent? What other interests do you have? What other activities do you or could you pursue?

2. What responsibilities are you letting your child neglect because you simply didn't have any fight left in you? What cheerleader friends can help you tackle that battlefront?

Closing Prayer

Lord God, I know all too well the natural tendency to fight against boundaries. I do that with you all the time, so it should come as no surprise that my kids fight boundaries as well. Guide me as I teach and model boundaries. Give me strength when my children test those boundaries, and grant me patience and compassion when they are angry and frustrated. And, Lord, show me what I can do to overcome obstacles to boundaries. Grant me the energy I need to persevere as the kids work to wear me down. Enable me to be boundaries for my kids so that they will grow into maturity that honors and glorifies you. I pray in Jesus' name. Amen.

Kid Kare at Home

1. Although by nature we resist limits from birth, we have a lot of help either developing boundaries or not developing them. What kind of help did you have at home either developing or not developing boundaries? In what ways did you respond—either defensively or responsibly—to the parenting you received in this area of boundaries? Give specific examples.

2. What kind of help has your child had so far either developing or not developing boundaries? In what ways is she responding—either defensively or responsibly—to the parenting you are offering in this area of boundaries?

angry and frustrated. And, Lord, show each one of us what we can do to overcome obstacles to boundaries. Grant us the energy we need to persevere as the kids work to wear us down. Even as you grow our own boundary building, enable us to be boundaries for our kids so that they—and we—will grow into maturity that honors and glorifies you. We pray in Jesus' name. Amen.

PLANNING NOTES

_____

_____

_____

_____

_____

_____

_____

_____

_____

_____

_____

Closing Prayer

Lord God, I know all too well the natural tendency to fight against boundaries. I do that with you all the time, so it should come as no surprise that my kids fight boundaries as well. Guide me as I teach and model boundaries. Give me strength when my children test those boundaries, and grant me patience and compassion when they are angry and frustrated. And, Lord, show me what I can do to overcome obstacles to boundaries. Grant me the energy I need to persevere as the kids work to wear me down. Enable me to be boundaries for my kids so that they will grow into maturity that honors and glorifies you. I pray in Jesus' name. Amen.

Kid Kare at Home

1. Although by nature we resist limits from birth, we have a lot of help either developing boundaries or not developing them. What kind of help did you have at home either developing or not developing boundaries? In what ways did you respond—either defensively or responsibly—to the parenting you received in this area of boundaries? Give specific examples.

2. What kind of help has your child had so far either developing or not developing boundaries? In what ways is she responding—either defensively or responsibly—to the parenting you are offering in this area of boundaries?

_____

_____

_____

_____

_____

_____

_____

_____

_____

_____

_____

_____

Session Three

Boundary Principles One and Two: The Law of Sowing and Reaping and the Law of Responsibility

BEFORE YOU LEAD

Key Points

- Life works on reality consequences. True change comes only when someone's behavior causes him to encounter reality consequences such as pain or losses of time, money, possessions, things he enjoys, or people he values. The Law of Sowing and Reaping depends on reality consequences.

- **The Law of Sowing and Reaping** teaches children self-control. They learn, "I am in control of the quality of my life. If I make good choices, life is better than if I don't."

- The formula for the Law of Sowing and Reaping is to give children freedom, to allow choices, and then to manage the consequences accordingly. Yet parents have difficulty allowing their children to suffer consequences.

- In short, the recipe for a growing person is always grace plus truth over time. Give a person grace (unmerited favor) and truth (structure), and do that over time, and you have the greatest chance of the person growing into a person of good character.

- We believe in rewards for acquiring new skills and performing exceptionally. We do not believe in rewards for doing the age-appropriate requirements of civilized people (such as living skills) and doing what is expected (such as work).

- **The Law of Responsibility** teaches children that they are responsible for themselves and their struggles. Children need to know that their problems are their own problems, no one else's.

- A large part of boundary training involves helping kids understand that they must gradually take responsibility for their own problems and take ownership of their emotions, attitudes, and behaviors.

- A child needs to understand that *being unable* is different than *being uncomfortable*. What kids don't enjoy, they think they can't do. Kids often want us to solve their problems for them. We must frustrate this desire and build within them a sense that, while they are to ask for help in matters beyond them (transportation, opportunities to make money, crises), they are expected to handle many things on their own (grades, behavior, tasks).

- A child needs to learn the difference between *help* and *rescue*. He is responsible *for* himself. He is responsible *to* others.

Synopsis

The Law of Sowing and Reaping means life works on reality consequences. Psychological and relational consequences, such as getting angry, sending guilt messages, nagging, and withdrawing love, usually do not motivate people to change. True change comes only when someone's behavior causes him to encounter reality consequences such as pain or losses of time, money, possessions, things he enjoys, or people he values. The Law of Sowing and Reaping motivates good work and diligence, at the same time fostering a healthy fear of laziness, irresponsibility, and other character problems.

The Law of Sowing and Reaping teaches children self-control. They learn, "I am in control of the quality of my life." They realize they have a choice whether they are inside and miserable or outside and playing. The formula for the Law of Sowing and Reaping is to give children freedom, to allow choices, and then to manage the consequences accordingly. The particulars will change through life, but the Law of Sowing and Reaping is the same: "If I make good choices, life is better than if I don't."

The recipe for a growing person is always grace plus truth over time. Give a person grace (unmerited favor) and truth (structure), and do that over time, and you have the greatest chance of this person growing into a person of good character.

We believe in rewards for acquiring new skills and performing exceptionally. We do *not* believe in rewards for doing the age-appropriate requirements of civilized people (such as living skills) and doing what is expected (such as work). Be careful of giving children the attitude that they have to perform only when someone pays them for it. Instead, they need to learn that *they* will have to pay if they don't perform. The Law of Sowing and Reaping forces children to meet the demands of life or to experience pain. Do your children a favor and teach them to make friends with reality early in life.

The Law of Responsibility—our second boundary principle—teaches children the valuable boundary lesson that they are responsible for themselves and their struggles. Children need to know that their problems are their own problems, no one else's. The aspects of life for which your kids need to take responsibility are what we call their *treasures,* or things of great value. Part of that treasure is character—how we love, work, and serve. Some treasures for which a child needs to take ownership are his emotions, attitudes, and behaviors.

Two key concepts help kids learn the Law of Responsibility. First, the child needs to understand that *being unable* differs from *being uncomfortable.* Kids see these two concepts as one. What they don't enjoy, they think they can't do. Kids often want us to solve their problems for them. We must frustrate this desire and build within them a sense that, while they are to ask for help in matters beyond them (transportation, opportunities to make money, crises), they are expected to handle many things on their own (grades, behavior, tasks).

The second key lesson in your child's course on responsibility is learning the difference between help and rescue. He is responsible *for* himself; he is responsible *to* others. However, while he is to care about his family and friends and go out of his way to help them, responsibility dictates that he refrain from protecting them from the consequences of their own actions.

Session Outline (56 minutes)

   I. Introduction (10 minutes)
     A. Welcome (1 minute)
     B. Review and Overview (8 minutes)
     C. Opening Prayer (1 minute)
  II. Discovery (44 minutes)
     A. Video Segment: What Will Happen If I Do This? (8 minutes)
     B. Kid Talk: Learning Lessons from Reality Consequences (8 minutes)
     C. Kid Kare: Making Good the Law of Sowing and Reaping (5 minutes)
     D. Video Segment: Pulling My Own Wagon (8 minutes)
     E. Kid Talk: What Kids Need to Understand (10 minutes)
     F. Kid Kare: What Kids Need to Take Responsibility For (5 minutes)
 III. Wrap-up (2 minutes)

Recommended Reading

"What Will Happen If I Do This? The Law of Sowing and Reaping" and "Pulling My Own Wagon: The Law of Responsibility," chapters 4 and 5 in *Boundaries with Kids.*

Session Three

Boundary Principles One and Two: The Law of Sowing and Reaping and the Law of Responsibility

10 MINUTES INTRODUCTION

1 minute Welcome

> Call the group together and welcome the participants to Session 3: Boundary Principles One and Two: The Law of Sowing and Reaping and the Law of Responsibility.

Welcome back! I've thought of you often this week and wondered how your own boundary work was going. It's interesting, isn't it, how our kids can stretch us and force us to change and grow.

8 minutes Review and Overview

> Participant's Guide pages 45–46.

Before we get started, I want to hear about your time with your kids this week. We'll start with the fun stuff. Who did something with your child that you know he or she loves to do? How did it go? What was your son's or daughter's reaction to your invitation? In what ways has your time together affected your interaction with your child since then? What, if anything, surprised you about that one-on-one time?

PLANNING NOTES

_____

_____

_____

_____

_____

_____

_____

_____

_____

_____

_____

_____

_____

_____

_____

_____

_____

_____

_____

_____

_____

_____

_____

_____

Session Three

Boundary Principles One and Two: The Law of Sowing and Reaping and the Law of Responsibility

OVERVIEW

In this session, you will

- Consider that true change comes only when someone's behavior causes him to encounter reality consequences such as pain or losses of time, money, possessions, things he enjoys, or people he values. The Law of Sowing and Reaping depends on such reality consequences.

- Learn the formula for the Law of Sowing and Reaping: Give children freedom, allow choices, and then manage the consequences accordingly. The recipe for a growing person is always grace plus truth over time.

- See that the Law of Responsibility teaches children that they are responsible for themselves and their struggles as well as for their emotions, attitudes, and behavior. Children need to know that their problems are their own problems, no one else's.

45

46   *Boundaries with Kids Participant's Guide*

- Identify two key principles the child needs to understand: first, that *being unable* differs from *being uncomfortable* and, second, that he is responsible *for* himself and responsible *to* others (that is, the difference between *help* and *rescue*).

> Note: Be ready to share an anecdote from your own life.

Now to a harder part of your Kid Kare at Home assignment. You were asked to think about what you might be contributing to your children's misbehavior. For whom did a lightbulb go on about some of the behavioral dynamics in your home? What did you realize about your part in creating the problem of your kid's misbehavior?

> Note: Again, be ready to share an anecdote from your own life.

It's good for us parents to stop and consider what we are doing to encourage or even reward our children's misbehavior. We must take responsibility and work to change our ways so that our kids' behavior also improves.

Today we'll first see how the Law of Sowing and Reaping depends on reality consequences to bring about true change in a person. We will also learn how the Law of Responsibility teaches children that they are responsible for themselves and their struggles as well as their emotions, attitudes, and behavior.

Let's open with a word of prayer before we begin.

1 minute   *Opening Prayer*

Lord God, thank you for the ways you use our children in our lives to teach us lessons, to point out our sin and our weaknesses, and to keep us turning to you for wisdom and guidance. Thank you too for this curriculum, this tool to help us become better parents. Be with us now as we look at two boundary principles. We ask you to give us insight into our kids and the dynamics at home, creativity about how to apply these principles, and then the strength to follow through. As we learn to parent with an eye to the future, we find great comfort that you hold that future for us as well as for our children. We thank you for your sovereign rule over our lives. In Jesus' name. Amen.

56 MINUTES   DISCOVERY

8 minutes   *Video Segment: What Will Happen If I Do This?*

Our first video segment today is called What Will Happen If I Do This? Let's hear what Dr. Cloud has to say.

> Remind the participants that key points of the video segment can be found on pages 47 and 48 of the Participant's Guide if they would like to review them at a later time.

PLANNING NOTES

_____

_____

_____

_____

_____

_____

_____

_____

_____

_____

_____

_____

_____

_____

_____

_____

_____

_____

_____

_____

_____

_____

VIDEO SEGMENT
What Will Happen If I Do This?

- Life works on reality consequences. Psychological and relational consequences, such as getting angry, sending guilt messages, nagging, and withdrawing love, usually do not motivate people to change. True change comes only when someone's behavior causes her to encounter reality consequences such as pain or losses of time, money, possessions, things she enjoys, or people she values.

- The Law of Sowing and Reaping depends on reality consequences. If our kids never learn the Law of Sowing and Reaping, they will not have the motivation to do good work and be diligent, nor will they fear laziness, irresponsibility, and other character problems.

- The goal of parenting is not to control the child into doing what you want, to "make them." The goal is to give them the choice to do what they want and make it so painful to do the wrong thing that they will not want to do it.

- The Law of Sowing and Reaping teaches children self-control. They learn, "I am in control of the quality of my life. If I make good choices, life is better than if I don't." They realize they have a choice whether they are inside and miserable or outside and playing.

- The formula for the Law of Sowing and Reaping is to give children freedom, to allow choices, and then to manage the consequences accordingly. Heap on praise and increase the freedoms when children use responsibility well. When your children make bad choices, empathize with their loss. Avoid the "I told you so's."

- Parenting means giving freedom, requiring responsibility, rendering consequences, and being loving throughout. Freedom, responsibility, consequences, and love must all be held in balance. Yet parents often have difficulty allowing their children to suffer consequences. Parents must be comfortable with letting the child suffer (see Hebrews 12:11).

- In short, the recipe for a growing person is always grace (unmerited favor) plus truth (structure) over time. Grace includes support, resources, love, compassion, forgiveness, and all of the relational sides of God's nature. Truth is the structure of life; it tells us how we are supposed to live our lives and how life really works. "If Mom tells me it's good for me to do *a*, *b*, or *c*, then that must be reality in order for me to learn it." It is the parents' job to make real that reality that it's good to do *a*, *b*, or *c*. Then and only then is the truth *really* true.

- We believe in rewards for acquiring new skills and performing exceptionally. We do *not* believe in rewards for doing the age-appropriate requirements of civilized people (such as living skills) and doing what is expected (such as work). Be careful of giving children the attitude that they have to perform only when someone pays them for it. They need to learn that *they* are the ones who will have to pay if they don't perform.

View Video Segment: What Will Happen If I Do This?

8 minutes   ## Kid Talk: Learning Lessons from Reality Consequences

Participant's Guide pages 49–50.

Let's talk a bit more about learning lessons from reality consequences. Please turn to pages 49 and 50 of your Participant's Guide.

1. What did Susan do effectively that Sally didn't?

> Possible answers: Susan included consequences in her instructions about the household chores—and then she acted on them! Susan helped Jen see that she had made her choice. Sally pitched in to help Jason despite his decision to not do the chore she wanted him to do.

2. How do Susan's kids benefit from her willingness and ability to both identify and enforce consequences? What do they learn?

> Possible answers: Susan's kids learned that sowing irresponsibility reaps the consequent loss of something they value—and that is a lesson for life! Susan's kids paid for their mistakes and learned from them. Furthermore, these consequences helped Susan's kids learn that the given situation is the child's problem.

3. Think for a moment about whether you are more like Sally or Susan in your follow-through. What do you think keeps parents from being more like Susan?

> Possible answers: Parents want to be liked. Parents don't want their kids to be sad or disappointed. Parents aren't yet skilled or ready in the moment to outline effective reality consequences. And, as we see in the next question, parents have difficulty allowing their children to suffer consequences.

4. Parents have difficulty allowing their children to suffer consequences. The natural tendency is to bail them out. Let's take a look at the following two scenarios:

> Note: To make these scenarios come to life, you may want to consider asking for volunteers to read the lines of the mom and child.

PLANNING NOTES

_____

_____

_____

_____

_____

_____

_____

_____

_____

_____

_____

_____

_____

_____

_____

_____

_____

_____

_____

_____

_____

_____

_____

_____

KID TALK
Learning Lessons from Reality Consequences

1. What did Susan do effectively that Sally didn't?

2. How do Susan's kids benefit from her willingness and ability to both identify and enforce consequences? What do they learn?

3. Think for a moment about whether you are more like Sally or Susan in your follow-through. What do you think keeps parents from being more like Susan?

4. Parents have difficulty allowing their children to suffer consequences. The natural tendency is to bail them out. Let's take a look at the following two scenarios.

SCENARIO #1

"Mom, I need some glue for my project."
"Sorry, dear. We don't have any."
"But I have to have it. The project is due tomorrow."
"When did you know about this assignment?"
"Two weeks ago."
"Why didn't you get the glue before now?"
"I forgot."
"The nearest store open this late is twenty minutes away. How could you do this to me?"

"I'm sorry, Mom. But I have to have it done or I'll get a bad grade."
"Okay, get in the car."

SCENARIO #2

"Mom, I need some glue for my project."
"Sorry, dear. I don't have any."
"But I have to have it. The project is due tomorrow."
"What teacher would call and give you an assignment at this hour without enough time to get the supplies?"
"Come on, Mom. She gave it to us at school."
"When?"
"Two weeks ago."
"Oh, so you've had two weeks to get glue and your other supplies?"
"Yes, but I thought we had them."
"Oh, that's sad. Seems like I remember this happening with the felt you needed for your last project. Well, I don't have any glue, and it's past my bedtime. I hope you figure out something to make that doesn't require glue. Good night, honey. I'm pulling for you."

What was your initial reaction to Mom number one? To Mom number two?

What, if anything, keeps you from regularly being a Mom number two? What are you afraid of? Why do you interrupt consequences before they teach your child a lesson for life?

Scenario #1

"Mom, I need some glue for my project."

"Sorry, dear. We don't have any."

"But I have to have it. The project is due tomorrow."

"When did you know about this assignment?"

"Two weeks ago."

"Why didn't you get the glue before now?"

"I forgot."

"The nearest store open this late is twenty minutes away. How could you do this to me?"

"I'm sorry, Mom. But I have to have it done or I'll get a bad grade."

"Okay, get in the car."

Scenario #2

"Mom, I need some glue for my project."

"Sorry, dear. I don't have any."

"But I have to have it. The project is due tomorrow."

"What teacher would call and give you an assignment at this hour without enough time to get the supplies?"

"Come on, Mom. She gave it to us at school."

"When?"

"Two weeks ago."

"Oh. So you've had two weeks to get glue and your other supplies?"

"Yes, but I thought we had them."

"Oh. That's sad. Seems like I remember this happening with the felt you needed for your last project. Well, I don't have any glue, and it's past my bedtime. I hope you figure out something to make that doesn't require glue. Good night, honey. I'm pulling for you."

- What was your initial reaction to Mom number one? To Mom number two?

- What, if anything, keeps you from regularly being a Mom number two? What are you afraid of? Why do you interrupt consequences before they teach your child a lesson for life?

If you find it difficult to allow your child to suffer consequences, be sure to find someone to help you work through your own resistance. Now let's turn to pages 51 and 52 in your Participant's Guide.

5 minutes

Kid Kare: Making Good the Law of Sowing and Reaping

Participant's Guide pages 51–52.

PLANNING NOTES

_____

_____

_____

_____

_____

_____

_____

_____

_____

_____

_____

_____

_____

_____

_____

_____

_____

_____

_____

_____

_____

_____

KID TALK
Learning Lessons from Reality Consequences

1. What did Susan do effectively that Sally didn't?

2. How do Susan's kids benefit from her willingness and ability to both identify and enforce consequences? What do they learn?

3. Think for a moment about whether you are more like Sally or Susan in your follow-through. What do you think keeps parents from being more like Susan?

4. Parents have difficulty allowing their children to suffer consequences. The natural tendency is to bail them out. Let's take a look at the following two scenarios.

SCENARIO #1

"Mom, I need some glue for my project."
"Sorry, dear. We don't have any."
"But I have to have it. The project is due tomorrow."
"When did you know about this assignment?"
"Two weeks ago."
"Why didn't you get the glue before now?"
"I forgot."
"The nearest store open this late is twenty minutes away. How could you do this to me?"

"I'm sorry, Mom. But I have to have it done or I'll get a bad grade."
"Okay, get in the car."

SCENARIO #2

"Mom, I need some glue for my project."
"Sorry, dear. I don't have any."
"But I have to have it. The project is due tomorrow."
"What teacher would call and give you an assignment at this hour without enough time to get the supplies?"
"Come on, Mom. She gave it to us at school."
"When?"
"Two weeks ago."
"Oh, so you've had two weeks to get glue and your other supplies?"
"Yes, but I thought we had them."
"Oh, that's sad. Seems like I remember this happening with the felt you needed for your last project. Well, I don't have any glue, and it's past my bedtime. I hope you figure out something to make that doesn't require glue. Good night, honey. I'm pulling for you."

What was your initial reaction to Mom number one? To Mom number two?

What, if anything, keeps you from regularly being a Mom number two? What are you afraid of? Why do you interrupt consequences before they teach your child a lesson for life?

The list of reality consequences is endless. The only limit is your own creativity.

Directions

Consider again the following principles for determining reality consequences. Working alone or with your spouse, you'll have 5 minutes to start this exercise, which you'll be able to finish at home. Any questions?

> Let the participants know when there is 1 minute remaining. Call the group back together after 5 minutes.

The Law of Sowing and Reaping—as difficult as it may be for parents to enact—relies on reality consequences to teach kids that they are responsible for themselves. The Law of Responsibility expands that definition of what kids are responsible for.

8 minutes   *Video Segment: Pulling My Own Wagon*

Dr. Cloud closed our first video with the statement "Do your children a favor and teach them to make friends with reality early in life. It is cheaper and safer—and your dinners will begin on time!" To make friends with reality, your children must learn to be responsible for the right things. What those things are is the topic of the next video.

> Remind the participants that key points of the video segment can be found on pages 53–55 of the Participant's Guide if they would like to review them at a later time.

> View Video Segment: Pulling My Own Wagon.

10 minutes   *Kid Kare: What Kids Need to Understand*

> Participant's Guide pages 56–57.

Let's consider further the two important principles—"It's Hard" vs. "I Can't" and Loving vs. Rescuing.

Directions

Please divide into groups of 3 or 4 and answer the questions found on pages 56 and 57 in your Participant's Guide. Make sure that everyone in your group has a chance to participate in the discussion. You will have 10 minutes to complete this exercise. Any questions?

PLANNING NOTES

_____

_____

_____

_____

_____

_____

_____

_____

_____

_____

_____

Session Three: Boundary Principles One and Two   51

KID KARE
Making Good the Law of Sowing and Reaping

The list of reality consequences is endless. The only limit is your own creativity.

DIRECTIONS

Consider again the following principles for determining reality consequences. Working alone or with your spouse, you'll have 5 minutes to start this exercise, which you'll be able to finish at home.

Make the consequences a natural outflow of the crime.

In what recent or recurring parenting situation will you incorporate natural consequences to teach the Law of Sowing and Reaping? Be specific about the consequences and how you will present them. Who will support you as you stand behind the consequences you establish?

Save consequences for serious offenses where the behavior may become a bad character pattern.

What serious offenses may be on their way to becoming a bad character pattern and therefore qualify for consequences in your home?

Give immediate consequences.

Why is immediacy important—and what keeps you from responding immediately? What will you do to remove that barrier so you're ready next time?

Stay away from emotional consequences and effect reality consequences.

What benefits—long-term as well as short-term—come with reality consequences?

---

52   Boundaries with Kids Participant's Guide

Use relational consequences only if they concern your own feelings.

In what kind of situation in your home would relational consequences be logical or natural? Be specific.

Think of consequences as protecting yourself and the rest of the family from the behavior of the child.

In what current or ongoing parenting situation would letting consequences happen benefit your family as well as help the guilty party learn the Law of Sowing and Reaping?

Preserve choice as much as possible.

Why is preserving a child's choice important? Why is it difficult to do so?

Make sure there is not a good reason a child is misbehaving before invoking consequences.

What are some "good reasons" for misbehavior that parents would be wise to be alert for?

Talk to the child and ask about the misbehavior when the child is not misbehaving.

When have you learned something important by talking with your child about her misbehavior when she is not misbehaving? Why do you tend to talk more in the heat of the moment than when it might be more helpful?

Session Three: Boundary Principles One and Two   53

VIDEO SEGMENT
Pulling My Own Wagon

- Children need to learn that they are responsible for themselves and their struggles. Children need to know that their problems are their own problems, no one else's. Their life is their own little red wagon, and their job is to pull it without expecting someone else to.

- A large part of boundary training with your kids will have to do with helping them understand that they must gradually take responsibility for their own problems.

- The aspects of life for which your kids must take responsibility we call their *treasures*, or things of great value. Part of that treasure is a person's character—how they love, work, and serve. Your child also needs to take ownership of his emotions, attitudes, and behavior.

- Children can learn to feel their emotions but not let the emotion carry them out of control.

- Parents can help children see the consequences of their attitudes and how they need to take responsibility for them.

- Children must learn that how they act is their responsibility. Children, however, link their emotions to their actions with no intervening agents such as thoughts, values, or empathy for others. As a parent, we must make it more painful for our child to be impulsive than to restrain behaviors. Children can learn that while they can't always control how they react emotionally, they can control how they respond behaviorally.

---

54   Boundaries with Kids Participant's Guide

- Another aspect of learning to take responsibility for oneself is for the child to understand that *being unable* differs from *being uncomfortable*. Kids see the two concepts as one. What they don't enjoy, they think they can't do. Since they can't do something they are uncomfortable doing, someone else will end up doing it—and that someone else is often the boundaryless parent.

- Part of growing up is learning what we are responsible for and what we need the help of others to do. According to Galatians 6, we should bear for one another the overwhelming "boulders" (burdens) in life, but we are to carry our own "knapsacks" (loads). Knapsacks are the normal responsibilities of working, going to school, and fulfilling duties to our friends, family, and church. Kids often see their "knapsacks" as "boulders" and want us to solve their problems for them. We must frustrate this desire and build within them a sense that, while they are to ask for help in matters beyond them (transportation, opportunities to make money, crises), they are expected to handle many things on their own (grades, behavior, tasks).

- Finally, through teaching the concept of responsibility, a child learns the difference between loving and rescuing. Your child is responsible *for* himself; he is responsible *to* others. While he is to care about his family and friends and go out of his way to help them, responsibility dictates that he refrain from protecting them from the consequences of their own actions.

- Our children's social groups offer other opportunities for learning about responsibility. It is, for example, hard for kids to withstand the intense social pressure not to tell about a friend who is into drugs

---

Session Three: Boundary Principles One and Two   55

or cheats on exams. They also benefit from learning how to say no to their friends' demands to solve their problems, take care of their feelings, and make them happy. A major reason children rescue is that they have learned it is the only way to keep a friend.

- It's easy to slip into allowing a child to rescue and become confused about responsibility, so be careful not to burden your children with your hurts. Your child has enough work to do in growing up. At the same time, learn the balance between helping him not to rescue but how to attend to the genuine needs of his family and friends.

---

56   Boundaries with Kids Participant's Guide

KID KARE
What Kids Need to Understand

DIRECTIONS

Within your group, take 10 minutes to answer the questions found below. Make sure that everyone in your group has a chance to participate in the discussion.

1. When have you seen your child conclude that being uncomfortable meant being unable? What did she decide she couldn't do because she was uncomfortable doing it?

2. What did you do in response to her "I can't" conclusion? What, if anything, would you like to do differently in a similar situation next time?

3. What are your kids asking for help with these days—boulders or their own knapsacks? How are you responding to their requests?

4. What are you doing to teach your kids that it's okay to ask for help and that none of us can live life alone?

Session Three: Boundary Principles One and Two   57

5. When, if ever, have you seen your child act as if she is responsible *for* her friends and not just *to* them?

> Let the participants know when there is 1 minute remaining. Call the group back together after 10 minutes.

I hope you were able to learn from each other during your discussion. Now let's turn to a final exercise regarding responsibility. Please turn to pages 58 through 61 in your Participant's Guide.

5 minutes   ## Kid Kare: What Kids Need to Take Responsibility For

> Participant's Guide pages 58–61.

Directions

Kids need to take responsibility for their emotions, their attitudes, and their behavior. The following exercise will help you get a sense of how well your kids are doing. Take 5 minutes to begin answering the questions. If you're here with your spouse, answer the questions together. Any questions?

> Let the participants know when there is 1 minute remaining. Call the group back together after 5 minutes.

2 MINUTES   # WRAP-UP

> Participant's Guide pages 62–65.

The Law of Sowing and Reaping and the Law of Responsibility are valuable concepts your kids can definitely start learning now. I look forward to talking with you next week to see how one or both of these principles will have impacted your parenting in the next seven days. Don't forget to take a look at the Kid Kare at Home ideas on pages 62 through 65 of your Participant's Guide. Spend some time with those if you can.

Now let's close in prayer.

Closing Prayer

Lord God, this parenting is a tough assignment. We're glad we can turn to you for guidance and help, for strength and perseverance. Please help us teach our kids that if they make good choices, life is better than if they don't. Enable us to give them grace and truth over time so you can build in them character that will glorify you. We ask for patience with the process and courage to let our kids face the consequences of their actions and decisions. We also ask you to supply us

PLANNING NOTES

_____

_____

_____

_____

_____

_____

58　　*Boundaries with Kids Participant's Guide*

KID KARE
What Kids Need to Take Responsibility For

DIRECTIONS

Kids need to take responsibility for their emotions, their attitudes, and their behavior, and we parents need to take responsibility for doing the parenting rather than letting our kids parent us. The following exercise will help you get a sense of how well your kids and you are doing. Take 5 minutes to begin answering the questions. If you're here with your spouse, answer the questions together.

EMOTIONS

Like all of us adults, children benefit from learning to use feelings in the ways for which God created them: as signals about the state of our soul.

1. Which emotions, if any, do you personally have trouble taking ownership of and/or controlling in a healthy way? What will you do to resolve this and thereby improve what you are modeling for your children?

2. Which emotions do your kids seem to have particular difficulty managing? What might you do to help them? Consider the following scenario:

Cheryl was at the end of her rope. Eleven-year-old Nathan threw tantrums when he was frustrated. Tantrums at that age could be scary. He would yell at her, stomp, slam doors, and sometimes throw things. Yet Cheryl thought, *He needs a place to let out those bottled-up feelings, or they'll eat him up inside.* So she continued to let Nathan "express himself" or she would try to soothe

---

Session Three: Boundary Principles One and Two　　59

and calm him. Unfortunately, his behavior escalated over time. Finally a friend told her, "You're training him to be a rageaholic." Stunned, Cheryl got some advice and changed her approach.

Cheryl told Nathan, "I know things make you angry, and I feel for your frustration. Things do get to all of us. But your feelings are disturbing me and the rest of the family. So here's what we've come up with. When you're mad, you can tell us you're angry. We want you to be honest with your feelings. And if it's about us, we will sit down and try to resolve the problem. But yelling, cursing, stomping, and throwing aren't acceptable. If those happen, you'll go to your room without phone, computer, or music until you can be civil. Then, for the minutes that you've disrupted the family, you'll need to do that many extra minutes of housework. I hope we can help you with these feelings."

Nathan didn't believe Cheryl at first. He escalated his disruptive behavior for a while, but Cheryl followed through on the consequences. After his initial period of protest, Nathan settled down and began to be master of his emotions. He began to identify the source of his anger and solve whatever problem in life had led to it. Nathan was beginning to own one of his treasures: his feelings.

ATTITUDES

We can help our children see the consequences of their attitudes and how they need to take responsibility for them.

1. What attitudes do you see each of your children taking toward the following?

Self (strengths and weaknesses, likes and dislikes)

Role in the family

60　　*Boundaries with Kids Participant's Guide*

Friends

God (who he is and how to relate to him)

School (their interests and duties)

Work

Moral issues (sex, drugs, gangs)

2. What red flags, if any, do you see in your answers? What will you do about those attitudes?

3. When kids have a problem, they (like adults) benefit from learning to examine what they may have done to contribute to the problem. What will you do this week to teach or reinforce this principle in your home?

BEHAVIOR

Children learn to conduct themselves in private and in public through love, teaching, modeling, and experiences. They need to learn that how they act is their responsibility.

1. Children link their emotions to their actions with no intervening agents such as thoughts, values, or empathy for others. They have no sense of, "What might happen if I act on my feelings?" What behaviors have you seen in your children that support this assertion? Give one or two examples.

Session Three: Boundary Principles One and Two　　61

2. As a parent, make it more painful for your child to be impulsive than to restrain behaviors. Also, build intervening agents into children by utilizing the concepts of validation, instruction, and experience. In what current situation in your home can you apply these three steps? Plan your strategy below. Be specific. Have someone hold you accountable for implementing your strategy.

Validation: Let them know their feelings are real and authentic, whether or not they are realistic.

Instruction: Tell them that acting on their anger or desire isn't appropriate. Give them ways to deal with their feelings, such as talking or substituting how you get what you need (for example, you get more privileges when respectful than when demanding).

Experience: Give them consequences for the behavior if it's still appropriate, and praise them when they take more ownership of their behavior.

WHO'S THE PARENT?

1. It's easy to slip into allowing a child to rescue and become confused about responsibility. When, if ever, have you seen someone parent a parent? How did that role affect that person's other relationships?

2. How, if at all, are you letting your children parent you? What needs, if any, are you inappropriately looking to your children to meet? Who is a better person for you to turn to—or where could you find a healthy, safe friend?

62　　*Boundaries with Kids Participant's Guide*

Closing Prayer

Lord God, this parenting is a tough assignment. I'm glad I can turn to you for guidance and help, for strength and perseverance. Please help me teach my kids that if they make good choices, life is better than if they don't. Enable me to give them grace and truth over time so you can build in them character that will glorify you. I ask for patience with the process and courage to let my kids face the consequences of their actions and decisions. I also ask you to supply me with wisdom as I teach my kids the difference between being responsible to others and responsible for oneself—and keep me from burdening my kids with any sense that they are responsible for me. I ask you to give me courage, this time to let my kids be uncomfortable as they learn and grow. And, Lord, I can't pray about these laws for my kids without praying for myself, that you would continue to teach me to live by the Law of Sowing and Reaping and the Law of Responsibility. I pray in Jesus' name. Amen.

Kid Kare at Home

1. Finish the Kid Kare exercises you started during the session.

The Law of Sowing and Reaping

Consequences transfer the need to be responsible from the parent to the child. Too many times, a child's behavior does not become a problem for her because it doesn't cost her things she values. Instead, parents allow the child's problem to become a problem for them. Consequences teach a child, "Too bad for me." They help him realize, "My behavior becomes a problem for me."

Session Three: Boundary Principles One and Two　　63

2. Think back over the last week or two. In what situation with your child did you carry the worry, strain, and effort rather than letting the problem be his? What problem are you currently carrying rather than letting it be your child's?

3. Consider what you did to keep your child from experiencing the problem as his own. What will you do next time to help him experience the problem as his? Or what will you do to let go of the situation that isn't yours to deal with? Who will help you follow through on your commitment to let your child's problem not be your problem?

4. Consider the ages of your kids. What choices does each one face regularly? In each situation, what are some appropriate consequences for them to have to manage if they make a poor choice? What additional privileges could result from your kids' good choices?

The Law of Responsibility

According to Galatians 6, we should bear for one another the overwhelming "boulders" (burdens) in life, but we need to carry our own "knapsacks" (loads). Knapsacks are the normal responsibilities of working, going to school, and fulfilling duties to our friends, family, and church. Kids often see their knapsacks as boulders and want us to

---

64　　*Boundaries with Kids Participant's Guide*

solve their problems for them. We need to frustrate this desire and build within them a sense that, while they are to ask for help in matters beyond them (transportation, opportunities to make money, crises), they are expected to handle many things on their own (grades, behavior, tasks). Consider the following opportunities for kids to learn responsibility:

Being honest and humble enough to realize you have a problem instead of being proud or denying the problem

Taking the initiative to ask for help from others instead of withdrawing or hoping it will go away

Picking trustworthy people of character you can ask for help

Doing your part to solve the problem

Valuing and appreciating the help that's given

Learning from experiences so that you don't repeat them

5. What are your children learning about these tasks from your modeling?

6. In what areas have you seen your kids demonstrate that they are tackling these tasks?

7. What will you do to help them with the other tasks?

Session Three: Boundary Principles One and Two　　65

BETWEEN SESSIONS READING

"What Will Happen If I Do This? The Law of Sowing and Reaping" and "Pulling My Own Wagon: The Law of Responsibility" chapters 4 and 5 in *Boundaries with Kids*.

with wisdom as we teach our kids the difference between being responsible to others and responsible for oneself—and keep us from burdening our kids with any sense that they are responsible for us. We ask you to give us courage, this time to let our kids be uncomfortable as they learn and grow. And, Lord, we can't pray about these laws for our kids without praying for ourselves, that you would continue to teach us to live by the Law of Sowing and Reaping and the Law of Responsibility. We pray in Jesus' name. Amen.

PLANNING NOTES

_____

_____

_____

_____

_____

_____

_____

_____

_____

_____

_____

---

62   *Boundaries with Kids Participant's Guide*

Closing Prayer

Lord God, this parenting is a tough assignment. I'm glad I can turn to you for guidance and help, for strength and perseverance. Please help me teach my kids that if they make good choices, life is better than if they don't. Enable me to give them grace and truth over time so you can build in them character that will glorify you. I ask for patience with the process and courage to let my kids face the consequences of their actions and decisions. I also ask you to supply me with wisdom as I teach my kids the difference between being responsible to others and responsible for oneself—and keep me from burdening my kids with any sense that they are responsible for me. I ask you to give me courage, this time to let my kids be uncomfortable as they learn and grow. And, Lord, I can't pray about these laws for my kids without praying for myself, that you would continue to teach me to live by the Law of Sowing and Reaping and the Law of Responsibility. I pray in Jesus' name. Amen.

Kid Kare at Home

1. Finish the Kid Kare exercises you started during the session.

The Law of Sowing and Reaping

Consequences transfer the need to be responsible from the parent to the child. Too many times, a child's behavior does not become a problem for her because it doesn't cost her things she values. Instead, parents allow the child's problem to become a problem for them. Consequences teach a child, "Too bad for me." They help him realize, "My behavior becomes a problem for me."

Session Four

Boundary Principles Three and Four: The Laws of Power and Respect

BEFORE YOU LEAD

Key Points

- **The Law of Power**—If parents don't get in the way, kids run into the reality that they don't have as much power as they thought. They adapt to reality rather than demanding that reality adapt to them.

- To develop appropriate boundaries, children need to have power, or the ability to control something. As a parent, your job is to help your children sort out what they do and don't have control of and the extent of their power.

- Five principles of power development can help parents gradually increase their child's power over himself and decrease his attempts to control his parents and others.

- **The Law of Respect**—To respect the boundaries of others and to get along with others, children must learn

  to not be hurtful to others;
  to respect the no of others without punishing them;
  to respect limits in general;
  to relish others' separateness; and
  to feel sad instead of mad when others' boundaries prevent them from getting what they want.

- It is normal for disrespect to occur, but it is not normal for it to continue. The cure is empathy and correction, then consequences.

- Another important aspect of respect is respecting separateness from the people we love. Allow children their own separateness. Give them age-appropriate freedom. Do not overstep their privacy and space when doing so is not necessary.

- People who are shown respect are the ones who have the greatest chance of learning respect.

Synopsis

The Law of Power—As a parent, your job is to help your children sort out what they do and don't have control of and the extent of their power. After all, children who grow up hanging on to their omnipotence and never coming to terms with their absolute failure may have difficulty seeing the need for a Savior.

In this session's first Kid Kare section, you'll talk about four important aspects of what children need to learn about power over themselves. They need, first, to stop denying dependency and realize that mature, healthy people need other people and God. Second, children need to stop demanding power over all choices and realize that their omnipotent illusion of unlimited time and energy is false. Third, they need to stop avoiding consequences and learn to prevent bad consequences by taking control of their actions. And, fourth, they have to stop avoiding failure: They need to learn to grieve their lost perfection, accept their failures, learn from them, and grow.

As you help your child give up his delusions of being able to perfectly control himself without failure, you will also need to help him with his similar delusions concerning his power over others. However, it is also important to help him see that, even though he can't have power over others, he isn't helpless, either. Your child needs to learn that he can influence others toward whatever he thinks is important.

Five principles of power development can help parents gradually increase their child's power over himself and decrease his attempts to control his parents and others:

1. Stay connected, no matter what.

2. Don't be an omnipotent parent.

3. Be a parent who makes free decisions.

4. Work toward giving your child self-governing power.

5. Limit omnipotence, but encourage autonomy.

The Law of Respect—But what does a parent do when her child uses his power to intrude on the boundaries of others? Respect for others' existence, needs, choices, and feelings does not come naturally. It's learned. Your task as a parent is to cure your child of this natural disrespect for the boundaries of other people.

To respect the boundaries of others and to get along with others, children must learn several things:

1. To not be hurtful to others

2. To respect the no of others without punishing them

3. To respect limits in general

4. To relish others' separateness

5. To feel sad instead of mad when others' boundaries prevent them from getting what they want

A child does not come into the world doing any of these five behaviors, so your work as a parent is cut out for you.

Normal children naturally hate limits when you first set them. But while it is normal for disrespect to occur, it is not normal for it to continue. The cure is empathy and correction, then consequences. When a parent's correction is followed by a child's apology, sufficient self-correction, and repentance, the child learns respect. If the child does not apologize, repent, and correct himself, or if this is a pattern, consequences should follow.

When your child is disrespectful, make sure you stay in control of yourself, as this is what boundaries are all about. Three things need to happen in such a situation:

1. You will not subject yourself to abuse.

2. Your child learns that his behavior hurts other people.

3. If the behavior is not self-correcting, it has to cost the child something.

A limit is generally not loved the first time around—or, for that matter, the first several times around! We protest limits. They limit our wish to be God. When you say no to children, they not only lose out on something they want, but they also find out that they are not in control of the universe. It's normal for children to protest limits. The problem arises when you get caught up in the protest. You may feel as if you either have to defend the limit or punish the protest. Neither option is very helpful. Remember, *the limit is reality if you keep it*.

Another important aspect of respect is respecting separateness from the people we love. Allow children their own separateness. To teach them to respect yours, you must respect theirs. Give them age-appropriate freedom.

Finally, the Law of Respect teaches children that the world does not belong to only them and that they have to share it with others. The path looks like this:

1. Children protest the limit.

2. They try to change the limit and punish the one setting it.

3. You hold to the limit, applying reality and offering empathy.

4. Children accept the limit and develop a more loving attitude toward it.

Session Outline (55 minutes)

I. Introduction (10 minutes)
   A. Welcome (1 minute)
   B. Review and Overview (8 minutes)
   C. Opening Prayer (1 minute)

II. Discovery (38 minutes)
  A. Video Segment: I Can't Do It All, But I'm Not Helpless, Either (7 minutes)
  B. Kid Talk: Power and Children (5 minutes)
  C. Kid Kare: Power over Myself (5 minutes)
  D. Video Segment: I'm Not the Only One Who Matters (6 minutes)
  E. Kid Talk: Respecting Limits (5 minutes)
  F. Kid Kare: Respecting Separateness (10 minutes)
III. Wrap-up (2 minutes)

Recommended Reading

"I Can't Do It All, But I'm Not Helpless, Either: The Law of Power" and "I'm Not the Only One Who Matters: The Law of Respect," chapters 6 and 7 in *Boundaries with Kids*.

Session Four

Boundary Principles Three and Four: The Laws of Power and Respect

<u>10 MINUTES</u> INTRODUCTION

1 minute   *Welcome*

> Call the group together and welcome the participants to Session 4: Boundary Principles Three and Four: The Laws of Power and Respect.

Welcome back! I'm looking forward to hearing how you've seen the first two laws of boundaries working in your home this week.

8 minutes   *Review and Overview*

> Participant's Guide Page 67.

As we review, let's first discuss the Law of Sowing and Reaping. Who was able to use consequences this week to make a problem your child's problem rather than your problem?

> Note: Be ready to share an anecdote from your own life.

We also talked about the Law of Responsibility last week, about boulders and knapsacks and about what kids can learn when they're dealing with a boulder. Who had the opportunity to remind a child that his knapsacks are normal responsibilities that you expect him to handle on his own? What did you do to remind him?

> Note: Be ready to share an anecdote from your own life.

PLANNING NOTES

_____

_____

_____

_____

_____

_____

_____

_____

_____

_____

_____

Session Four

Boundary Principles Three and Four: The Laws of Power and Respect

OVERVIEW

In this session, you will

- See that, according to the Law of Power, if parents don't get in the way, kids run into the reality that they don't have as much power as they thought.

- Identify four realizations that, as children make them, help them come to terms with their limited power over themselves.

- Look at five principles of power development that can help parents gradually increase their child's power over himself and decrease his attempts to control his parents and others.

- Learn about the Law of Respect and see that the cure for disrespect is empathy and correction, then consequences.

- Be encouraged to allow children their own separateness, to give them age-appropriate freedom, and to not overstep their privacy and space when doing so is not necessary.

- Consider five goals of the Law of Respect.

67

_____

_____

_____

_____

_____

_____

_____

_____

_____

_____

_____

_____

_____

We also talked about a child's six jobs when she is dealing with a boulder: being honest and humble enough to realize you have a problem; taking the initiative to ask for help; picking trustworthy people of character to help you; doing your part to solve the problem; valuing and appreciating the help you receive; and learning from your experience so you don't repeat it. Whose child was dealing with an actual boulder? Which of these jobs did you see her doing?

> Note: Be ready to share an anecdote from your own life.

→ Today we're going to move on to two more boundary principles. First, according to the Law of Power, if parents don't get in the way, kids realize they don't have as much power as they thought. Also, the Law of Respect states that the cure for disrespect is empathy and correction, then consequences.

We'll begin with a video segment from Dr. Cloud and Dr. Townsend, but first let's take a moment to pray.

1 minute   *Opening Prayer*

Thank you, Father God, that you are our perfect parent and that, by your Spirit, you are always with us to guide in the multitude of split-second decisions we need to make in the course of a day. Thank you that the universe you designed runs according to a cause-and-effect principle that enables us to learn from the consequences of our actions and that we parents can let the consequences of our children's actions be their teachers. Thank you, too, that you are always there for us as we deal with the boulders as well as the knapsacks in our life. Finally, thank you that you are here with us now as we look at two more principles that can help us be more the parents you call us to be. Open our hearts to your truth, bless our discussion, and guide us as we learn to parent. We pray in Jesus' name. Amen.

38 MINUTES DISCOVERY

7 minutes   *Video Segment: I Can't Do It All, But I'm Not Helpless, Either*

> Remind the participants that key points of the video segment can be found on pages 68–70 of the Participant's Guide if they would like to review them at a later time.

PLANNING NOTES

_____

_____

_____

_____

_____

_____

_____

_____

_____

_____

_____

_____

_____

_____

_____

_____

_____

Session Four

Boundary Principles Three and Four: The Laws of Power and Respect

OVERVIEW

In this session, you will

- See that, according to the Law of Power, if parents don't get in the way, kids run into the reality that they don't have as much power as they thought.
- Identify four realizations that, as children make them, help them come to terms with their limited power over themselves.
- Look at five principles of power development that can help parents gradually increase their child's power over himself and decrease his attempts to control his parents and others.
- Learn about the Law of Respect and see that the cure for disrespect is empathy and correction, then consequences.
- Be encouraged to allow children their own separateness, to give them age-appropriate freedom, and to not overstep their privacy and space when doing so is not necessary.
- Consider five goals of the Law of Respect.

67

---

68   *Boundaries with Kids Participant's Guide*

VIDEO SEGMENT
I Can't Do It All, But I'm Not Helpless, Either

- At some time or another, children think they are grown up, strong, and without limitations. If parents don't get in the way, kids run into the reality that they don't have as much power as they thought. They adapt to reality rather than demanding that reality adapt to them.
- To develop appropriate boundaries, children need to have power, or the ability to control something. As a parent, your job is to help your children sort out what they do and don't have control of and the extent of their power.
- Children who grow up hanging on to their omnipotence and never coming to terms with their absolute failure may have difficulty seeing the need for a Savior.
- Children come to terms with their limited power over themselves when they stop denying dependency and learn that mature, healthy people need other people and God; demanding power over all choices and realize their omnipotent illusion of unlimited time and energy is false; avoiding consequences and learn to prevent bad consequences by taking control of their actions; and avoiding failure and learn to grieve their lost perfection, accept their failures, learn from them, and grow.
- Along with delusions of being able to perfectly control himself without failure, your child has similar delusions concerning his power over others. Whether due to fear or a desire to be God, children think they have power over their family and friends.
- A child may feel sad that she can't rule her relational world. However, help her see that even though she

---

Session Four: *Boundary Principles Three and Four*   69

can't have power over others, she isn't helpless either. Your child needs to learn that she can influence others toward whatever she thinks is important.

- Five principles of power development can help parents gradually increase their child's power over himself and decrease his attempts to control his parents and others.

  1. **Stay connected, no matter what.** Empathize with her fears of being helpless, her frustration that she can't control her friends' reactions, and her concerns about failure.
  2. **Don't be an omnipotent parent.** Admit your failure, weakness, and limitations—but own what power you do have. The statement "I can't make you stop, but I can tell you what will happen if you don't" is a helpful parenting tool.
  3. **Be a parent who makes free decisions.** Be a parent whose choices aren't dictated by your child's responses. His feelings and desires matter to you because you love him, but you are the boss. The key is not to *need* anything such as appreciation, support, respect, or understanding from your child. Get those needs met elsewhere.
  4. **Work toward giving your child self-governing power.** The challenge is to know what you can let your child handle that takes him out of his comfort zone but is not beyond his maturity. Stretch but don't break him.
  5. **Limit omnipotence, but encourage autonomy.** Your job as a parent is to gradually increase your child's power over himself and decrease his attempts to control you and others.

- Your child needs the power that comes from a realistic sense of self-control (healing power), and she needs to

---

70   *Boundaries with Kids Participant's Guide*

give up the desire to have absolute power over herself and her relationships (harmful power). A reality-based understanding of power will provide her with a foundation for respecting, setting, and keeping boundaries.

_____

_____

_____

_____

_____

_____

_____

_____

| View Video Segment: I Can't Do It All, But I'm Not Helpless, Either. |

Keep in mind those five principles of power development. They can help us parents gradually increase our child's power over himself and decrease his attempts to control his parents and others. Let's take some time now to discuss further the concept of children and power. Please turn to page 71 in your Participant's Guide.

5 minutes

Kid Talk: Power and Children

| Participant's Guide page 71. |

1. Describe the ideal power balance between a parent and a child. Who should have what kind of power?

| Possible answers: The ideal power balance between a parent and a child is determined by the age and maturity of the child. The child should, as much as possible, have power and choices over as much of her life as she can handle without serious problems. The parent handles the rest, with the idea being that over time, as she matures, the parent gradually hands the reins of power over her decisions to her, for that is her adult destiny. |

2. In what areas does each of your children enjoy a certain amount of power?

| Possible answers: Choosing between two or three extracurricular options; deciding what to wear; offering ideas about how to decorate or arrange the bedroom. Putting a puzzle together, dancing in a recital, solving a conflict, or developing a friendship. |

3. What do your children do when they face something they can't control?

problem solve
finally and politely

| Note: Be ready to share an anecdote from your own family (scream, cry quietly, pout, etc.). |

4. An infant and her parents illustrate the paradox of kids and power. Why would an infant argue that she has no power?

| Possible answers: She wavers between unpleasant states of terror, helplessness, and rage and pleasant states of safety, warmth, and love. The infant has no power over herself. |

PLANNING NOTES

_____

_____

_____

_____

_____

_____

_____

_____

_____

_____

_____

KID TALK
Power and Children

1. Describe the ideal power balance between a parent and a child. Who should have what kind of power?

2. In what areas does each of your children enjoy a certain amount of power?

3. What do your children do when they face something they can't control?

4. An infant and her parents illustrate the paradox of kids and power. Why would an infant argue that she has no power?

5. What specific evidence would her parents use to argue that the infant does indeed exert power in the family?

_____

_____

_____

_____

_____

_____

_____

_____

_____

_____

_____

_____

_____

5. What specific evidence would an infant's parents use to argue that the infant does indeed exert power in the family?

> Possible answers: Mom and Dad rearrange their work schedules, home life, and sleeping routines around their new baby. They carry her gently and are careful about germs. They install a monitor in her bedroom to make sure she is breathing.

The infant is powerless, yet she paradoxically wields significant control over her parents! As she grows up, she will more consciously assume and exert power over herself. She'll come to understand what she can and can't do regarding herself. This next exercise will help you see our role in that growth.

Please turn to pages 72 through 74 in your Participant's Guide.

10 minutes *Kid Kare: Power over Myself*

> Participant's Guide pages 72–74.

Directions

We will be doing this exercise in 4 small groups. You will have 5 minutes to discuss a pair of questions found on pages 72 and 73. Take time this week to look over the other three topics. Any questions?

> Let the group know when there is 1 minute remaining. Call the group back together after 5 minutes.

As Dr. Townsend said at the end of the first video, our children need "the power that comes from a realistic sense of self-control . . . and [they] need to give up the desire to have absolute power. A reality-based understanding of power will provide kids with a foundation for respecting, setting, and keeping boundaries." But what does a parent do when her child uses his power to intrude on the boundaries of others? We'll deal with this now as we address the Law of Respect.

6 minutes *Video Segment: I'm Not the Only One Who Matters*

> Remind the participants that key points of the video segment can be found on pages 75–76 of the Participant's Guide if they would like to review them at a later time.

PLANNING NOTES

KID TALK
Power and Children

1. Describe the ideal power balance between a parent and a child. Who should have what kind of power?

2. In what areas does each of your children enjoy a certain amount of power?

3. What do your children do when they face something they can't control?

4. An infant and her parents illustrate the paradox of kids and power. Why would an infant argue that she has no power?

5. What specific evidence would her parents use to argue that the infant does indeed exert power in the family?

KID KARE
Power over Myself

DIRECTIONS

Take 5 minutes to discuss the assigned pair of questions found below. Take time this week to look over the other three topics.

STOP DENYING DEPENDENCY

Two kinds of dependency often get confused here. *Functional dependency* relates to the child's resistance to doing the tasks and jobs in life that are his responsibility. *Relational dependency* is our need for connectedness to God and others. It is crucial to discourage the former and encourage the latter.

1. What are you doing to discourage functional dependency? What consequences are you allowing your child to deal with so that he learns the importance of taking responsibility for himself? (Who is supporting you as you enforce these consequences?)

2. What are you doing to encourage relational dependency? Start by noting which of the following are already part of your parenting repertoire. Under "Other," note any different strategies you may have developed.
   - Confronting isolation
   - Waiting until you are invited to help
   - Encouraging him to express his wants, needs, and opinions
   - Recognizing and respecting his own rhythm of when he needs to be close and when he needs distance from you
   - Not being intrusive and affectionate when he clearly needs to be more separate
   - Not abandoning him when he needs more intimacy

   - Encouraging him to share his feedback on family activities
   - Other:

STOP DEMANDING POWER OVER ALL CHOICES

Children think they have the power to do everything they set their mind to. No activity level is too much. They have an omnipotent illusion of their unlimited time and energy. Your child needs your help in this. They can develop boundary problems by over-committing themselves.

1. Has your child overcommitted herself, trying to put too many activities into too little time? What evidence of this do you see?

2. What system have you or could you set up that will break down if she does too much? Consider factoring in such age-appropriate requirements as an acceptable grade point average in school, four nights at home with the family each week, an established bedtime, and no signs of fatigue or stress.

STOP AVOIDING CONSEQUENCES

Part of your "little angel's" makeup is a criminal mind. He thinks he's powerful enough to avoid the results of his actions. Kids will manipulate, lie, rationalize, and distort to avoid punishment.

1. When have you recently seen evidence of your little angel's criminal mind at work? Give an example. How did you respond?

---

2. What are the consequences for dishonesty in your home? What do you do to reward honesty and encourage your child to admit when she has disobeyed?

STOP AVOIDING FAILURE

Born perfectionists, kids don't like to be reminded that they are products of the Fall. They often think they have the power to avoid making mistakes or failing. Your child needs to learn to grieve his lost perfection, accept his failures, learn from them, and grow.

1. Think about how you deal with failure. What are you modeling for your kids? What would you like them to be seeing?

2. Which of your mistakes or failures are your kids well aware of? Why is it important that they know, for instance, about the traffic ticket you got?

> View Video Segment: I'm Not the Only One Who Matters.

Please turn to page 77 of your Participant's Guide and explore this issue of respecting limits a bit more.

5 minutes   ## *Kid Talk: Respecting Limits*

> Participant's Guide page 77.

As we know from the video, if not already from our own experience, it's normal for children to protest limits. The problem arises when you, the parent, get caught up in the protest. You feel as if you either have to defend the limit or punish the protest. Neither option is very helpful. Remember, *the limit is reality if you keep it*.

1. Explain why, if you argue with or condemn your protesting child, you become the problem.

> Possible answers: The child focuses on you rather than the limit you want to set. She rejects the reality internally, and she hates you since you are now the enemy.

2. What did Mom not do in her discussion with her daughter who wanted to go to the movies? What life lessons did she teach here?

> Possible answers: Mom does not explain, defend, or shame for the "pain of the moment." She keeps the limit and empathizes with how her daughter is feeling. Mom offers love and limits rather than harshness, punishment, or something for her daughter to argue about. Mom has held the limits—a lesson for life. She has also let her daughter's problem remain her daughter's problem.

3. Why is it important that limits are enforced with love?

> Possible answers: Love and limits together enable kids to internalize the reality of limits in a nonadversarial way. Plus, if you argue with or condemn a child, he has no loving parent to help him deal with reality.

4. When protesting limits, your child wants reality to change and he wants you to feel the pain he's feeling. Why is it not wise to let the reality change?

> Possible answers: You don't want to teach a child of any age that enough protest changes reality.

PLANNING NOTES

_____

_____

_____

_____

_____

_____

_____

_____

_____

_____

_____

_____

_____

_____

VIDEO SEGMENT
I'm Not the Only One Who Matters

- Respect for other people's existence, needs, choices, and feelings does not come naturally to children.

- To respect the boundaries of others and to get along with others, children must learn several things:

  To not be hurtful to others

  To respect the no of others without punishing them

  To respect limits in general

  To relish others' separateness

  To feel sad instead of mad when others' boundaries prevent them from getting what they want

- It is normal for disrespect to occur, but it is not normal for it to continue. The cure is empathy and correction, then consequences. When a parent's correction is followed by a child's apology, sufficient self-correction, and repentance, the child learns respect. If the child does not apologize, repent, and correct himself or if this is a pattern, consequences should follow.

- When your child is disrespectful, make sure you stay in control of yourself. Three things need to happen in such a situation:

  1. You will not subject yourself to abuse.
  2. Your child learns that his behavior hurts other people.
  3. If the behavior is not self-correcting, it has to cost the child something.

- It is normal for children to protest limits. The problem arises when you get caught up in the protest. You feel as if you either have to defend the limit or

---

  punish the protest. Neither option is very helpful. Remember, the limit is reality if you keep it.

- Another important aspect of respect is respecting separateness from the people we love. Allow children their own separateness. Give them age-appropriate freedom. Do not overstep their privacy and space when you don't need to.

- People who are shown respect are the ones who have the greatest chance of learning respect.

- The Law of Respect teaches children that the world does not belong only to them, but that they have to share it with others. It teaches that they must learn to treat their neighbors as they want to be treated; that they won't always get things their way, and that they need to be okay when they don't. It teaches that they must learn to tolerate not being able to move a limit, that they should be able to hear no from others without a fight, and that they must allow others to have lives separate from them.

- The path toward these results looks like this:

  1. Children protest the limit.
  2. They try to change the limit and punish the one setting it.
  3. You hold to the limit, applying reality and offering empathy.
  4. Children accept the limit and develop a more loving attitude toward it.

KID TALK
Respecting Limits

1. Explain why, if you argue with or condemn your protesting child, you become the problem.

2. What did Mom not do in her discussion with her daughter who wanted to go to the movies? What life lessons did she teach here?

3. Why is it important that limits are enforced with love?

4. When protesting limits, your child wants reality to change and he wants you to feel the pain he's feeling. Why is it not wise to let the reality change?

5. Why is it important to let him know you are aware of his pain?

5. Why is it important to let him know you are aware of his pain?

> Possible answers: Choosing empathy can keep you from becoming angry or punitive. Empathy can also help the child begin to feel sadness as she faces the reality of your limits.

Just as kids need to learn to respect limits—something they do as you offer them limits and love—they also need to learn separateness. That's the topic of our next discussion. Please turn to pages 78 and 79 in your Participant's Guide.

10 minutes   *Kid Kare: Respecting Separateness*

> Participant's Guide pages 78–79.

Directions

Please form small groups of 3 or 4 people. You will have 10 minutes to discuss the questions found on pages 78–79 and talk about the fact that your kids need separation from you and you need separation from them. Any questions?

> Let the participants know when there is 1 minute remaining. Call the group back together after 10 minutes.

2 MINUTES   WRAP-UP

> Participant's Guide pages 80–84.

Before we close in prayer, let me remind you that this week's Kid Kare at Home questions are on pages 80 through 84 of your Participant's Guide. You'll be encouraged to finish answering the Power over Myself and Respecting Separateness questions. There's also a very helpful chart with suggestions about how you can respond when your kids try to have power over you. You'll also consider the goals of the Law of Respect. And it's always extra credit—and extra benefit for your relationship with your kids—to do something unexpected and fun with one of your kids. Of course, make sure that the "fun" is defined by your son or daughter!

Now let's pray.

PLANNING NOTES

_____

_____

_____

_____

_____

_____

_____

_____

_____

_____

_____

_____

_____

---

78   *Boundaries with Kids Participant's Guide*

KID KARE
Respecting Separateness

DIRECTIONS

In your small group, take 10 minutes to discuss the questions found below and talk about the fact that your kids need separation from you and you need separation from them.

KIDS NEED SEPARATENESS TOO

Allow children their own separateness. To teach them to respect yours, you have to respect theirs. Give them age-appropriate freedom and do not require them to be at your side at all times. Do not overstep their privacy and space when doing so is not necessary.

1. What limits are reasonable for each aspect of life listed below? What consequences do you or will you enforce if those limits aren't honored? Be specific for each child.

• Their space. (Consider safety, common areas in the home, and lost items.)

• Their time. How will you teach that time limits (mealtimes, the beginning of school, scheduled outings) are real?

• Their choice of friends. What will you say to your child about friends they are choosing that you would not choose for them? If your children's choice of friends is dangerous, you have to act. What will you do?

Session Four: *Boundary Principles Three and Four*   79

• Their money. What can you do and *not* do to help your children learn about financial responsibility?

• Their clothing and appearance. Why are clothes and hairstyles that are *not putting your child in danger* not worth fighting for?

YOUR SEPARATENESS FROM THEM

In addition to your children's separateness from you, you have to be separate from them. Parents who do not have a life apart from their kids teach the kids that the universe revolves around them.

1. What evidence do your children see that you have a life of your own?

2. In what ways do both you and your child benefit from that separateness?

---

80   *Boundaries with Kids Participant's Guide*

Closing Prayer

Father, thank you for today's encouraging words about how understanding the Law of Power and the Law of Respect can help me be a better parent. Help me, Lord, to let my kids encounter and confront the reality that they don't have as much power as they thought. Give me courage and creativity and the strength to be consistent as I work, by the power of your Spirit, to gradually increase my child's power over himself and decrease his attempts to control his parents and others.

I ask you to grant me compassion and wisdom that I may be truly empathic and effective as I correct and, when necessary, outline consequences when my kids are disrespectful. Help me to allow children their own separateness and to give them age-appropriate freedom.

Help me, Lord, to be a parent who stays connected, whatever power issues my kids are dealing with, and acts respectfully toward others. To you be the glory as I put into action these biblical principles in my attempt to raise my kids to love you and serve you. In Jesus' name. Amen.

Kid Kare at Home

1. Finish the Kid Kare exercises you began in this session.

2. Read through the following chart for suggestions about how you can respond when your kids try to have power over you. Which response do you expect to be able to use this week as your child attempts to have power over you? Watch for the opportunity and note the effect of your words.

Session Four: *Boundary Principles Three and Four*   81

Attempt to Have Power over Others	Your Response
If I whine long enough, I'll get the toy.	Ask me once, and I'll decide. But whining gets an automatic no.
I can push my friends around.	They seem to avoid you now. Let's hold off on inviting people until you and I deal with this by coaching you on how to treat people.
If I am polite and helpful, I won't have to stay on restriction for my last curfew violation.	I'm glad your attitude is good, but you are in for the duration of your sentence.
I can ignore your requests to clean up the family room.	I won't ask more than once, and you have fifteen minutes. After that, you miss the game with your friends.
I can intimidate you with my yelling and anger.	Your rage does bother me, and it's a big deal. So until you can be appropriate and talk to me respectfully, all privileges are suspended.

---

82   *Boundaries with Kids Participant's Guide*

| My hatred can destroy you. | You can make me uncomfortable and hurt my feelings. But your hatred doesn't injure me or make me go away. |

3. People who are shown respect are the ones who have the greatest chance of learning respect. You can't ask for your children what you aren't willing to give to them. The five goals of the Law of Respect are listed below. The questions that accompany them will help you determine how well you are obeying the Law of Respect—and what you're teaching your kids about respect.

• *Don't hurt others.* When you hurt your children, do you own the behavior and apologize? Do you tell them you were just thinking of yourself and you're sorry? Do you ask for their forgiveness? If these will be new behaviors, practice formulating those words now—and find someone who can hold you accountable to apologizing to your kids when you hurt them.

• *Respect the no of others without punishing them.* When your spouse or children say no to something you want, do you punish them by anger, manipulation, or withdrawal of love? Do you allow your children to say no to you in matters they should have freedom in? Do you give them choices about managing their own lives? If you want them to play baseball but they like soccer, are they free to say no to you? What if they do not agree with you on all

---

Session Four: *Boundary Principles Three and Four*   83

your thoughts about God? Are they free to have separate opinions about their faith?

• *Respect limits in general.* How do you deal with limits in general? Do you always try to "get around" the rules—and are you modeling that for your children? Do you accept appropriate limits or are you teaching your children that rules are good for everyone except you?

• *Relish others' separateness.* Do you relish the separateness of others? Are they allowed to have a life apart from you? Are you allowing your children to grow in independence and separateness from you? Do you love their freedom or hate it?

• *Feel sad instead of mad when you don't always get what you want.* When you don't get what you want from your children or others, do you get angry or sad? Do you protest their choices with anger or accept them with sadness? When things do not go your way, do you throw a temper tantrum or do you feel sad and then move on?

---

84   *Boundaries with Kids Participant's Guide*

4. What does the above inventory reveal to you about yourself? What growth would you like to pursue? What steps will you take to become more respectful? Whom will you ask to hold you accountable in your efforts?

5. Do something unexpected and fun with one of your kids. Of course, make sure that the fun is defined by your son or daughter!

BETWEEN SESSIONS READING

"I Can't Do It All, But I'm Not Helpless, Either: The Law of Power" and "I'm Not the Only One Who Matters: The Law of Respect," chapters 6 and 7 in *Boundaries with Kids*.

Closing Prayer

Father, thank you for today's encouraging words about how understanding the Law of Power and the Law of Respect can help us be better parents. Help us, Lord, to let our kids encounter and confront the reality that they don't have as much power as they thought. Give us courage and creativity and the strength to be consistent as we work, by the power of your Spirit, to gradually increase our child's power over himself and decrease his attempts to control his parents and others.

We ask you to grant us compassion and wisdom that we may be truly empathic and effective as we correct and, when necessary, outline consequences when our kids are disrespectful. Help us to allow children their own separateness and to give them age-appropriate freedom.

Help us, Lord, to be parents who stay connected, whatever power issues our kids are dealing with, and parents who act respectfully toward others. To you be the glory as we put into action these biblical principles in our attempt to raise our kids to love you and serve you. In Jesus' name. Amen.

PLANNING NOTES

_____

_____

_____

_____

_____

_____

_____

_____

_____

_____

_____

Closing Prayer

Father, thank you for today's encouraging words about how understanding the Law of Power and the Law of Respect can help me be a better parent. Help me, Lord, to let my kids encounter and confront the reality that they don't have as much power as they thought. Give me courage and creativity and the strength to be consistent as I work, by the power of your Spirit, to gradually increase my child's power over himself and decrease his attempts to control his parents and others.

I ask you to grant me compassion and wisdom that I may be truly empathic and effective as I correct and, when necessary, outline consequences when my kids are disrespectful. Help me to allow children their own separateness and to give them age-appropriate freedom.

Help me, Lord, to be a parent who stays connected, whatever power issues my kids are dealing with, and acts respectfully toward others. To you be the glory as I put into action these biblical principles in my attempt to raise my kids to love you and serve you. In Jesus' name. Amen.

Kid Kare at Home

1. Finish the Kid Kare exercises you began in this session.

2. Read through the following chart for suggestions about how you can respond when your kids try to have power over you. Which response do you expect to be able to use this week as your child attempts to have power over you? Watch for the opportunity and note the effect of your words.

Session Five

Boundary Principles Five and Six: The Laws of Motivation and Evaluation

BEFORE YOU LEAD

Key Points

- **The Law of Motivation**—Motives drive our behavior. Motives are the internal "because" behind the external actions we perform. We all want our kids to do the right things for the right reasons.

- Many parents rant, rave, and threaten, and the kids stay in line as long as the parents are standing over them. But such behavior, dictated from the outside, marks a child, not a young adult.

- Sending guilt messages or threatening a loss of love never pays off in the long run. Appeals to improper motives not only do not work but also hurt your child.

- As a parent, you want to develop in the soul of your child a desire to do the right things and to avoid the wrong ones because of empathic concern for others and a healthy respect for the demands of God's reality.

- How do you help your children develop good motivation? First, realize that your child needs to be rooted and grounded in love (see Ephesians 3:17). So love first, set limits second.

- Healthy motivation develops in these four stages: fear of consequences; an immature conscience; values and ethics; and mature love and mature guilt.

- Your child needs to be concerned about the pain of consequences of irresponsibility, the rights and wrongs of his behavior, and what pain his actions may cause his friends and God.

- **The Law of Evaluation**—The effective parent must learn the distinction between *hurt* and *harm* if a child is ever going to develop boundaries. Harm refers to any actual injury by wounding the child's person, judging, attacking, abandoning, or otherwise not providing something she needs.

- Lesson number one in parenting and life is "Growth involves pain." Lesson number two is "Not all pain produces growth."

- When your child does cry or complain, keep in mind these four rules for evaluating his pain.

  Rule #1: Don't let your child's pain control your actions.
  Rule #2: Keep your pain separate from your child's.
  Rule #3: Help your child see that life is not about avoiding pain but about making good pain an ally.
  Rule #4: Make sure the pain is the pain of maturing, not the pain of need or injury.

- Struggle refines a child's character. Waiting for the reward makes a child learn how to perform. Trials and pain teach us the lessons that build the character we will need to negotiate life.

Synopsis

Motives drive our behavior. Motives are the internal "because" behind the external actions we perform. Motives develop in stages in a child's character. We all want our kids to do the right things for the right reasons. But how does a parent help a child develop the right motive for love and good works?

As a parent, you want to develop in the soul of your child a desire to do the right things and to avoid the wrong ones because of empathic concern for others and a healthy respect for the demands of God's reality. But how do you help your children develop good motivation? God has hardwired several stages of influences through which you will guide your children. Before you start learning about these four stages, however, realize that your child needs to be rooted and grounded in love (Ephesians 3:17). Only when you stay connected to her can she grow. Only when she knows that you love her can learning occur. So love first, set limits second, and you'll see motives develop in these stages:

1. Fear of consequences

2. An immature conscience

3. Values and ethics

4. Mature love, mature guilt

Your child needs to be concerned about the pain of consequences of irresponsibility, the rights and wrongs of his behavior, and what pain his actions may cause his friends and God.

The effective parent must learn the distinction between *hurt* and *harm* if a child is ever going to develop boundaries. Harm means actual injury by wounding her person, judging, attacking, abandoning, or otherwise not providing something she needs. Lesson number one in parenting and life is "Growth involves pain." Lesson number two is "Not all pain produces growth." Learning to tell the difference is the key to having someone stay on the bottom or grow past where he or she is. When your child does cry or complain, keep in mind these four rules for evaluating his pain.

> Rule #1: Don't let your child's pain control your actions.
> Rule #2: Keep your pain separate from your child's.
> Rule #3: Help your child see that life is not about avoiding pain but about making good pain an ally.
> Rule #4: Make sure the pain is the pain of maturing, not the pain of need or injury.

God does not rescue us from our struggles and the pain of learning discipline and perseverance. In fact, God disciplines those he loves, just as a father disciplines his children (Hebrews 12:5–10). Besides, struggle refines the character of the child. Waiting for the reward makes a child learn how to perform. Trials and pain teach us the lessons that build the character we will need to negotiate life.

So evaluate your child's pain. If she is in need or injured, run to her rescue. But if she is protesting reality's demands for maturing to the next level, empathize with that struggle, manage it well, but let her go through it to the end. Later, she will thank you.

Session Outline (56 minutes)

> I. Introduction (10 minutes)
>   A. Welcome (1 minute)
>   B. Review and Overview (8 minutes)
>   C. Opening Prayer (1 minute)
> II. Discovery (45 minutes)
>   A. Video Segment: Life Beyond "Because I'm the Mommy" (7 minutes)
>   B. Kid Talk: Cheerfulness, Connectedness, and Persistence (8 minutes)
>   C. Kid Kare: Your Kid's Motives (7 minutes)
>   D. Video Segment: Pain Can Be a Gift (6 minutes)
>   E. Kid Talk: Count It All Joy (10 minutes)
>   F. Kid Kare: Four Rules for Evaluating Pain (7 minutes)
> III. Wrap-up (1 minute)

Recommended Reading

"Life Beyond 'Because I'm the Mommy': The Law of Motivation" and "Pain Can Be a Gift: The Law of Evaluation," chapters 8 and 9 in *Boundaries with Kids*.

Session Five

Boundary Principles Five and Six: The Laws of Motivation and Evaluation

10 MINUTES INTRODUCTION

1 minute   Welcome

> Call the group together and welcome the participants to Session 5: Boundary Principles Five and Six: The Laws of Motivation and Evaluation.

8 minutes   Review and Overview

> Participant's Guide Page 85.

We covered some important ground last week as we discussed the Law of Power and the Law of Respect, and I'd like to hear how it impacted your week at home.

First, who would like to talk about an opportunity to use one of the responses Dr. Cloud and Dr. Townsend suggested for those times when your child tries to have power over you?

> Note: Be ready to share an anecdote from your own life.

Who did something fun and creative with your child last week? We'd like to learn from you!

> Note: Be ready to share an anecdote from your own life.

PLANNING NOTES

_____

_____

_____

_____

_____

_____

_____

_____

_____

Session Five

Boundary Principles Five and Six: The Laws of Motivation and Evaluation

OVERVIEW

In this session, you will

- Recognize that healthy motivation is the desire to do the right things and to avoid the wrong ones because of empathic concern for others and because of a healthy respect for the demands of God's reality.

- Learn both how to help your child develop this good motivation and in what stages these motives develop.

- Acknowledge that your child needs to be concerned about the pain of consequences of irresponsibility, the rights and wrongs of his behavior, and what pain his actions may cause his friends and God.

- Be called to make the distinction between *hurt* and *harm*.

- Review four rules for evaluating your child's pain.

- Be reminded that God does not rescue us from our struggles and the pain of learning discipline and perseverance and that trials and pain teach us the lessons that build the character we will need to negotiate life.

85

Today we'll look at two more boundary principles: The Law of Motivation and the Law of Evaluation. First, healthy motivation is the desire to do the right things and to avoid the wrong ones because of empathic concern for others and a healthy respect for the demands of God's reality. We'll learn how to help kids develop this good motivation. Then, in the discussion of the Law of Evaluation, we'll be called to make the distinction between hurt and harm, and we'll review four rules for evaluating a child's pain.

Let's first open with a word of prayer.

1 minute   ## Opening Prayer

Lord God, even as we move on to the next two boundary principles, we know we've only begun to help our children with the Law of Power and the Law of Respect. Guide us as we teach them what they do and don't have power over, the extent of their power over the things they do control, and how to adapt to the things they can't control. And since people who are shown respect are the ones who have the greatest chance of learning respect, help us respect our children. Enable us to allow them their own separateness and to give them age-appropriate freedom. As always, these parenting tasks humble us and remind us of our need for you. Thank you for being Emmanuel, "God with us," as we parent. We pray in Jesus' name. Amen.

43 MINUTES   DISCOVERY

7 minutes   ## Video Segment: Life Beyond "Because I'm the Mommy"

> Remind the participants that key points of the video segment can be found on pages 86–87 of the Participant's Guide if they would like to review them at a later time.

> View Video Segment: Life Beyond "Because I'm the Mommy."

We parents sure do have our work cut out for us! It helps to get ideas from each other when the task seems so formidable. Please turn to page 88 of your Participant's Guide.

8 minutes   ## Kid Talk: Cheerfulness, Connectedness, and Persistence

> Participant's Guide page 88.

PLANNING NOTES

_____

_____

_____

_____

_____

_____

_____

_____

_____

_____

_____

_____

_____

Session Five

Boundary Principles Five and Six: The Laws of Motivation and Evaluation

OVERVIEW

In this session, you will

- Recognize that healthy motivation is the desire to do the right things and to avoid the wrong ones because of empathic concern for others and because of a healthy respect for the demands of God's reality.

- Learn both how to help your child develop this good motivation and in what stages these motives develop.

- Acknowledge that your child needs to be concerned about the pain of consequences of irresponsibility, the rights and wrongs of his behavior, and what pain his actions may cause his friends and God.

- Be called to make the distinction between *hurt* and *harm*.

- Review four rules for evaluating your child's pain.

- Be reminded that God does not rescue us from our struggles and the pain of learning discipline and perseverance and that trials and pain teach us the lessons that build the character we will need to negotiate life.

85

---

86   *Boundaries with Kids Participant's Guide*

VIDEO SEGMENT

Life Beyond "Because I'm the Mommy"

- Motives drive our behavior. Motives are the internal "because" behind the external actions we perform. And we all want our kids to do the right things for the right reasons.

- Many parents rant, rave, and threaten, and the kids stay in line as long as the parents are standing over them. But such behavior, dictated from the outside, marks a child, not a young adult.

- Sending guilt messages or threatening a loss of love never pays off in the long run. Appeals to improper motives not only do not work but also hurt your child.

- As a parent, you want to develop in the soul of your child a desire to do the right things and to avoid the wrong ones because of empathic concern for others and a healthy respect for the demands of God's reality.

- How do you help your children develop good motivation? First, realize that your child needs to be rooted and grounded in love (Ephesians 3:17). So love first, set limits second, and you'll see motives develop in the following stages:

  1. *Fear of consequences.* As you begin setting limits and consequences with your child, she will almost certainly test, protest, and express hatred. However, stick with your boundaries, be fair but consistent, and empathize with your child's emotional reactions. Helping your child develop a healthy fear of consequences aligns her with God's reality and makes that reality her friend instead of her nemesis.

Session Five: *Boundary Principles Five and Six*   87

2. *An immature conscience.* The next step involves a child internalizing his experiences with significant relationships and taking them into himself. Stay consistent, loving, and attentive to your child's changes. If you have a good enough attachment to your child and he has accepted your boundaries, then your boundaries will become his.

3. *Values and ethics.* At this stage of motive development, your child may begin asking many value-laden questions ("Is this a bad word?" or "Is it okay to watch this TV show?"). Be prepared for these kinds of questions and the opportunities they give you to explain why you believe what you believe about how people should conduct themselves in the world. As she continues to work out her own ethics, keep bringing your child back to reality principles like "That goes against what you and we believe."

4. *Mature love, mature guilt.* At this point the child moves and grows beyond the ethical questions of right and wrong to the highest motive: love. Once again, it is crucial that you avoid overcriticism or withdrawing love. Children who are internalizing boundaries need to move beyond "This is right or wrong" to "This hurts others or God." Your role is to help them freely choose who and how to love and to freely love.

- Your child needs to be concerned about the pain of consequences of irresponsibility, the rights and wrongs of his behavior, and what pain his actions may cause his friends and God.

1. The apostle Paul writes, "Let each one do just as he has purposed in his heart; not grudgingly or under compulsion; for God loves a cheerful giver" (2 Corinthians 9:7 NASB). What is the difference between being a cheerful giver as you do a certain task and enjoying that task? Where do your kids see you being a cheerful giver even though you don't particularly enjoy the task? What regular opportunities do your kids have to be cheerful givers?

Possible answers: Helping with household chores, giving an offering at church, walking a younger sibling to school, etc.

2. What can we parents do to stay connected to our kids not only in their joys and sorrows but also in their anger at and disappointment in us? Be specific. What are some empathic words for times when our kids are angry or disappointed?

Possible answers: Not getting angry in return, not being defensive, being empathetic.

"I understand how frustrating this must be for you." "I know. I hate it too when I have to work instead of doing things I want to do." "It's hard to miss something you were looking forward to."

3. One wise father said, "You have to stick to your guns one more time than the child. If he breaks the rule ten thousand times, you have to stay with it only ten thousand and one times, and you'll win." What do you do to maintain the stamina you need to hold the line? Who in your life encourages you and holds you accountable to your parenting goals?

Possible answers: Pray; be sure I'm eating right and sleeping enough; take time out for myself.

Maintaining the stamina we need to help our kids develop good, healthy motivation isn't easy. But one thing that might help is understanding a child's four stages of motive development. And that's what we'll look at now. Please turn to pages 89 and 90 in your Participant's Guide.

7 minutes   ## Kid Kare: Your Kid's Motives

Participant's Guide page 89–90.

PLANNING NOTES

_____

_____

_____

_____

_____

_____

_____

_____

_____

_____

_____

KID TALK
Cheerfulness, Connectedness, and Persistence

1. The apostle Paul writes, "Let each one do just as he has purposed in his heart; not grudgingly or under compulsion; for God loves a cheerful giver" (2 Corinthians 9:7 NASB). What is the difference between being a cheerful giver as you do a certain task and enjoying that task? Where do your kids see you being a cheerful giver even though you don't particularly enjoy the task? What regular opportunities do your kids have to be cheerful givers?

2. What can we parents do to stay connected to our kids not only in their joys and sorrows but also in their anger at and disappointment in us? Be specific. What are some empathic words for times when our kids are angry or disappointed?

3. One wise father said, "You have to stick to your guns one more time than the child. If he breaks the rule ten thousand times, you have to stay with it only ten thousand and one times, and you'll win." What do you do to maintain the stamina you need to hold the line? Who in your life encourages you and holds you accountable to your parenting goals?

_____

_____

_____

_____

_____

_____

_____

_____

_____

_____

_____

Directions

Alone or with your spouse, take the next 7 minutes to think about your kids, where they are in the four stages of motive development, and what you can do to help them along. Any questions?

> Let the participants know when there is 1 minute remaining. Call the group back together after 7 minutes.

This exercise probably has you wondering about how detached a parent you are, whether you tend to connect only when your child is good, or how well you are modeling right behavior. The Law of Evaluation gives us yet another idea to grapple with, namely, the reality that boundaries cause pain in our children. We need to learn whether the pain is helpful or harmful. This is the subject of the next video segment, Pain Can Be a Gift.

6 minutes   *Video Segment: Pain Can Be a Gift*

> Remind the participants that key points of the video segment can be found on pages 91–92 of the Participant's Guide if they would like to review them at a later time.

> View Video Segment: Pain Can Be a Gift.

Letting our kids hurt is a tough aspect of parenting, isn't it? Let's look at what the Bible says about suffering and think together about the suffering we've done. Please turn to page 93 in your Participant's Guide.

10 minutes   *Kid Talk: Consider It All Joy*

> Participant's Guide page 93.

James 1:2–4 reads, "Consider it pure joy, my brothers, whenever you face trials of many kinds, because you know that the testing of your faith develops perseverance. Perseverance must finish its work so that you may be mature and complete, not lacking anything."

God does not rescue us from our struggles and the pain of learning discipline and perseverance. In fact, God disciplines those he loves, just as a father disciplines his children (see Hebrews 12:5–10).

1. What lessons have you learned from the struggles of your life?

PLANNING NOTES

_____

_____

_____

_____

_____

_____

_____

_____

_____

_____

_____

_____

_____

_____

_____

_____

_____

_____

KID KARE
Your Kid's Motives

DIRECTIONS

Alone or with your spouse, take the next 7 minutes to think about your kids, where they are in the four stages of motive development, and what you can do to help them along.

1. Where is your child on the spectrum of obeying to avoid punishment and obeying because it's the right thing to do? Let "1" be behavior dictated by the outside, external restraints, and you the parent and "10" be owning behavior and doing the right things for the right reasons.

2. Detachment is one of the enemies of the kind of contact that enables your child to grow. Consider how detached a parent you are. Do you express your feelings of love for your child? Do you let yourself get close? If you answer no to these questions, where will you go to find supportive relationships in which you can learn to be vulnerable and accessible—and when will you go?

3. Conditional love is another enemy of the kind of parent-child contact that enables a child to grow. Are you connecting to your child only when he is good? Are you withdrawing when his behavior is bad? If your answer is yes, what will you do to break this pattern?

---

4. As a parent, you can express your awareness of the pain of consequences for your own irresponsibility, model right behavior, and acknowledge what pain your actions may cause for your friends and God. Even as all that is happening, create many experiences for your children to internalize these realities and own them for themselves. What opportunity for that internalization can you anticipate having this week? Be ready!

VIDEO SEGMENT
Pain Can Be a Gift

- The effective parent must learn the distinction between *hurt* and *harm* if a child is ever going to develop boundaries. Harm means any actual injury by wounding the child's person, judging, attacking, abandoning, or otherwise not providing something she needs.

- The first lesson in parenting and life is "Growth involves pain." Lesson number two is "Not all pain produces growth." Learning to tell the difference is the key to having someone stay on the bottom or grow past where he or she is.

- When your children do cry or complain, keep in mind these four rules for evaluating their pain:

  Rule #1: Don't let your child's pain control your actions. Frustration and painful moments of discipline help a child learn to delay gratification, one of the most important character traits a person can have.

  Rule #2: Keep your pain separate from your child's. We all must endure our own pain.

  Rule #3: Help your child see that life is not about avoiding pain but about making good pain an ally. Life is about learning to suffer well. We can learn from what a wise mom tells her son: "I know, Tim. Livin' is hard—but I believe you can do it."

  Rule #4: Make sure the pain is the pain of maturing, not the pain of need or injury. When you evaluate your child's pain, first make certain that it is not caused by a real injury or trauma or something other than the real need for discipline. Second,

---

make sure you have not caused the pain. Normal parents will cause pain from time to time, but they will see their fault and apologize.

- God does not rescue us from our struggles and the pain of learning discipline and perseverance. In fact, God disciplines those he loves, just as a father disciplines his children (see Hebrews 12:5–10).

- Struggle refines the child's character. Waiting for the reward makes a child learn how to perform. Trials and pain teach us the lessons that build the character we will need to negotiate life.

- Evaluate your child's pain. If they are in need or injured, run to their rescue. But if they are protesting reality's demands for maturing to the next level, empathize with that struggle, manage it well, but let them go through it to the end. Later, they will thank you.

KID TALK
Consider It All Joy

God does not rescue us from our struggles and the pain of learning discipline and perseverance. In fact, God disciplines those he loves, just as a father disciplines his children (see Hebrews 12:5–10).

1. What lessons have you learned from the struggles of your life?

2. What kind of pain have you experienced as you've learned discipline and perseverance?

3. In what specific situation are you currently struggling to allow your child to experience helpful pain, the kind of pain, for instance, that teaches discipline and perseverance? Why is it hard for you? What will you do to make it easier for you?

4. If you have caused some of your child's pain, have you gone to him or her to ask for forgiveness? If you have, briefly describe what happened. If you haven't, what's keeping you from doing so? You'll be surprised by your child's reaction to your request for forgiveness.

> Possible answers: Just because you're doing what God wants you to do doesn't mean the path will be easy. God meets us in our struggles. God's strength really is made perfect in our weakness.

2. What kind of pain have you experienced as you've learned discipline and perseverance?

> Possible answers: Frustration that a new skill does not come quickly or easily. Sadness about being the last one chosen for a team.

3. In what specific situation are you currently struggling to allow your child to experience helpful pain, the kind of pain, for instance, that teaches discipline and perseverance? Why is it hard for you? What will you do to make it easier for you?

> Possible answers: Time management in the morning before school starts: he will make himself late. Time management in the evening: she will either be tired from staying up late, or she won't get her homework finished.

4. If you have caused some of your child's pain, have you gone to him or her to ask for forgiveness? If you have, briefly describe what happened. If you haven't, what's keeping you from doing so? You'll be surprised by your child's reaction to your request for forgiveness.

So how do we know if our kids are being harmed or if the pain they're feeling is the pain of growth? Our next exercise will give you four rules for evaluating pain. Please turn to pages 94 through 97 in your Participant's Guide.

7 minutes   ## Kid Kare: Four Rules for Evaluating Pain

> Participant's Guide pages 94–97.

Directions

We will be doing this exercise in groups of four. Each group will be assigned a rule for evaluating pain. You can finish the rest of the exercise during the week. You will have 7 minutes to begin working on the following questions.

PLANNING NOTES

_____

_____

_____

_____

_____

_____

_____

_____

_____

_____

_____

_____

_____

_____

_____

_____

_____

_____

KID TALK
Consider It All Joy

God does not rescue us from our struggles and the pain of learning discipline and perseverance. In fact, God disciplines those he loves, just as a father disciplines his children (see Hebrews 12:5–10).

1. What lessons have you learned from the struggles of your life?

2. What kind of pain have you experienced as you've learned discipline and perseverance?

3. In what specific situation are you currently struggling to allow your child to experience helpful pain, the kind of pain, for instance, that teaches discipline and perseverance? Why is it hard for you? What will you do to make it easier for you?

4. If you have caused some of your child's pain, have you gone to him or her to ask for forgiveness? If you have, briefly describe what happened. If you haven't, what's keeping you from doing so? You'll be surprised by your child's reaction to your request for forgiveness.

KID KARE
Four Rules for Evaluating Pain

DIRECTIONS

We will be doing this exercise in groups of four. Each group will be assigned a rule for evaluating pain. You can finish the rest of the exercise during the week. You will have 7 minutes to begin working on the following questions.

Rule #1: Don't let your child's pain control your actions.

If your child is controlling your decisions by protesting your boundaries, you are no longer parenting with purpose. When a parent does not have self-control in enforcing the rules, a child will not develop self-control.

1. What are some of the lessons you teach your kids when you give in to their crying?

2. A child's protest does not define either reality or right from wrong. In what current parenting situation will this truth help you stand strong and empathize with your child's pain but enforce the limit? What will you say to express your empathy? Who will support you as you try to stand strong?

Frustration and painful moments of discipline help a child learn to delay gratification, one of the most important character traits a person can have. If you rescue your children from their anger at your boundary, you can plan on more anger at later limits.

Rule #2: Keep your pain separate from your child's.

1. Could you be overidentifying with your child's pain? Consider your own childhood and your reactions to your child's sadness. What specific interaction with your child suggests that you may be overidentifying?

2. If you are overidentifying, to whom will you turn for support as you learn to keep your experience separate from your child's? Who can remind you of the truth that your child's pain is not as intense as the pain you knew growing up?

Keep your own sadness about your children's pain separate from theirs. "Each heart knows its own bitterness, and no one else can share its joy" (Proverbs 14:10). We all must endure our own pain.

Rule #3: Help your child see that life is not about avoiding pain but about making good pain an ally.

Basically, we change when the pain of staying the same becomes greater than the pain of changing. Therefore, life is not about avoiding suffering; life is about learning to suffer well.

1. In teaching your children that pain can be good, which of the following have you been able to model recently or will you start modeling today? Be brief about the circumstances.

• Facing problems

• Being sad but continuing onward

• Empathizing with them about how hard it is to do the right thing and then still requiring it

2. What do you think your kids learned from how you handled the situation(s) you just identified?

Problems come from the tendency to avoid the pain of the momentary struggle, the pain of self-discipline and delaying gratification. If we learn to lose what we want in the moment, to feel sad instead of mad about not getting our way, and then to adapt to the reality demands of difficult situations, joy and success will follow.

Rule #4: Make sure the pain is the pain of maturing, not the pain of need or injury.

Children's behavior often sends a message, and parents need to evaluate the pain to find out if it is the pain of frustration or the pain of need or injury. A four-year-old may be dawdling not to defy her dad but because she is missing her mom.

1. Older children sometimes misbehave not only out of defiance or avoidance of reality but also for some of these valid reasons:

• Hurt feelings from parents and others

• Anger over feelings of powerlessness in a relationship and not having enough control over oneself

• Trauma, such as loss of a parent or abuse he may have suffered somewhere

• Medical and physical reasons

• Psychiatric problems, such as attention deficit disorder, depression, or thought disorders

---

• A recent change in the structure of the family, the schedule, or lifestyle

Which of these, if any, may explain some recent or ongoing misbehavior in your home?

2. Now consider whether you may be the source of your child's pain. Review the following list of things parents do to exasperate or embitter their kids (Ephesians 6:4; Colossians 3:21).

• Exercising too much control over your children's lives so they have no power over or choice in their lives

• Disciplining with anger and guilt instead of empathy and consequences

• Not meeting their needs for love, attention, and time

• Not affirming their successes, but only commenting on their failures

• Being too perfectionistic about their performance instead of being pleased with their effort and with the general direction in which they are going

What, if anything, have you done to exasperate your children or embitter them? If that hasn't happened, consider how your child may perceive or experience your regular interactions. Are you at risk of exasperating or embittering them? Who knows you well enough to help you answer that question if you're not sure? If your child's exasperation is either real or potential, what will you do today to improve the relationship?

When you evaluate your child's pain, make sure, first, that it is not caused by a real injury or trauma or something other than the real need for discipline and, second, that you have not caused it. Normal parents will cause pain from time to time, but they will see their fault and apologize.

> Let the participants know when there is 1 minute remaining. Call the group back together after 7 minutes.

1 MINUTE — WRAP-UP

> Participant's Guide pages 98–100.

The Law of Motivation and the Law of Evaluation—the truths we've learned about today are truths for life, for adults as well as for kids! May God bless you this week as you work on these laws as well as the Kid Kare at Home exercise you'll find on pages 98 through 100 of your Participant's Guide. Let's close in prayer now.

Closing Prayer

Lord God, teach us to love our children better! Use us to develop in the soul of these children you've entrusted to us a desire both to do the right things and to avoid the wrong ones. Please give us the wisdom to discern hurt versus harm, the strength to let our children hurt, and an eye to the future when the present seems full of tears, protests, and anger. Once again, we are thankful that we can turn to you as we try our best to care for and grow up these kids you've blessed us with. In Jesus' name. Amen.

PLANNING NOTES

_____

_____

_____

_____

_____

_____

_____

_____

_____

_____

_____

_____

_____

_____

_____

_____

_____

_____

---

98   *Boundaries with Kids Participant's Guide*

Closing Prayer

Lord God, teach me to love my children better! Use me to develop in the soul of these children you've entrusted to me a desire both to do the right things and to avoid the wrong ones. Please give me the wisdom to discern hurt versus harm, the strength to let my children hurt, and an eye to the future when the present seems full of tears, protests, and anger. Once again, I am thankful that I can turn to you as I try my best to care for and grow up these kids you've blessed me with. In Jesus' name. Amen.

Kid Kare at Home

1. Review Your Kid's Motives and finish Four Rules for Evaluating Pain.

The Law of Motivation

2. Your child needs to be concerned about the pain of consequences for irresponsibility, the rights and wrongs of his behavior, and what pain his actions may cause for his friends and God. What are you doing to teach these three motives for good behavior? List a few of your actions or statements by each.

   • The pain of consequences for irresponsibility

   • The rights and wrongs of his behavior

Session Five: *Boundary Principles Five and Six*   99

   • What pain his actions may cause for his friends and God

3. What kind of modeling are you doing? Be specific in each instance.

   • The pain of consequences for your own irresponsibility

   • Right behavior

   • Your consideration of what pain your actions may cause for your friends and God

Even as you model your own awareness of the pain of consequences for your irresponsibility, as you model right behavior, and as you consider and acknowledge what pain your actions may cause your friends and God, create many experiences for your child to internalize them and own them for himself.

The Law of Evaluation

4. Struggle refines the character of the child. Waiting for the reward makes a child learn how to perform. Trials and pain teach us the lessons that build the character we will need to negotiate life. What signs do you see, if any at this point, that life's struggles have removed or

---

100   *Boundaries with Kids Participant's Guide*

at least started to wear down some of your child's rough edges? Be specific about the struggles as well as their refining work in your child's character.

5. Tackle a project with your children at home (paint the backyard fence, clean up the garage, bake cookies) or in the community (serve at the local soup kitchen, mow the lawn for the family down the street whose father is sick, make a meal for a family that just had a baby, work in the church nursery on Sunday). The shared sense of accomplishment could be great for your relationship!

BETWEEN SESSIONS READING

"Life Beyond 'Because I'm the Mommy': The Law of Motivation" and "Pain Can Be a Gift: The Law of Evaluation," chapters 8 and 9 in *Boundaries with Kids*.

Session Six

Boundary Principles Seven and Eight: The Laws of Proactivity and Envy

BEFORE YOU LEAD

Key Points

- **The Law of Proactivity**—Reactive boundaries protect and help separate your child from bad things, but they are insufficient for a successful adult life.

- Proactive boundaries go beyond problem identification to problem solving. They encompass both what the child is for and against. Proactive boundaries mean others can't control the child. They are not about revenge and fairness but about responsibility

- Proactive boundaries encourage the child to solve problems, not just complain about them; help him define what he loves, not just what he hates; help him get out from under the control of others; and help him focus on getting his needs met instead of judging the world for not being fair to him.

- **The Law of Envy**—Envy is the perpetual "wanting more." Related to envy, entitlement is when someone feels as if people owe him things or special treatment simply because he exists. The opposite of entitlement and envy is gratitude. Gratitude comes from the feeling of freely receiving things, not because we deserve them, but because someone has graced us with them.

- The balance of gratification and frustration tempers the extremes of neediness and entitlement. A child learns to not see himself as a victim when he's deprived, nor does he see others as bad when they do not do what he wants. In order to give your children this balanced sense of themselves and others, you must gratify needs and some wants, and frustrate others. The three skills necessary to do this are giving, limiting, and containing.

- It's also important to tolerate being hated, to teach your children to express gratitude, and to distinguish between wishes that come from envy and wishes that are heartfelt.

Synopsis

The Law of Proactivity—The struggle between reactivity and proactivity, between lashing out in protest and responding maturely to problems, is a challenge in child rearing and boundaries that exists, at some level, in all of us. A parent's job is to help children develop the ability to set appropriate boundaries, yet without exploding or being impulsive.

The reality is, however, that reactive boundaries have their place in your child's development. First, children's reactive boundaries are necessary for their survival and growth. Children need to be able to protest what they are against, fear, or do not like. Being able to protest helps the child define herself, keep the good in and the bad out, and develop the ability to take responsibility for her own treasures. But protest merely identifies the problem, it doesn't solve it. Reactive boundaries signal that something needs to be dealt with, but it is proactive boundaries that fix something that is broken. Proactive boundaries lead to mature, loving boundaries through a sequence of abilities and skills.

Reactive boundaries protect and help separate your child from bad things, but they are insufficient for a successful adult life because children need to grow up to be defined by more than what they hate. Furthermore, children who never move beyond reactive boundaries develop a victim identity. They look at most of their struggles in life as coming from the outside, not from inside themselves. Thus, they are forever prohibited from improving their lives because no problem that originates outside of us is really solvable.

In contrast, proactive boundaries go beyond problem identification to problem solving. Proactive boundaries encompass both what the child is for and against. Proactive boundaries mean others can't control the child. Proactive boundaries are not about revenge and fairness but about responsibility.

Put differently, proactive boundaries encourage the child to solve problems, not just complain about them; help him define what he loves, not just what he hates; help get him out from under the control of others; and help him focus on getting his needs met, not judging the world for not being fair to him.

The Law of Envy—Envy is a perpetual "wanting more." Related to envy, entitlement is when someone feels as if people owe him things or special treatment simply because he exists. The opposite of entitlement and envy is gratitude. Gratitude comes from the feeling of freely receiving things, not because we deserve them, but because someone has graced us with them. Gratitude and envy have little to do with what a person actually receives; they have more to do with the character of the person. Parents must help children work through their feelings of entitlement and envy and move to a position of gratitude.

The balance of gratification and frustration tempers the extremes of neediness and entitlement. In addition, a child learns to not see himself as a victim when he's deprived, nor does he see others as bad when they do not do what he wants. He develops a balanced view of himself and others. In order to give your children this balanced sense of themselves and others, you must gratify needs and some wants, and frustrate others. The three skills necessary to do this are giving, limiting, and containing.

It's also important to tolerate being hated. While having love and the ability to set limits are important qualities for a parent, so is the ability to tolerate being hated and seen as "bad" by your child.

Expressing gratitude is another very important aspect of development. A child who is not expressing thanks is taking things for granted. Let him know this is not appreciated by others. Help your child learn to express gratitude by setting forth your own limits in not allowing yourself to be taken for granted.

Finally, determine which of your child's wishes come from envy and which are heartfelt desires. Desire moves our children (and us) to work. Envy just burns within. Envious people think they deserve everything, but in the end have nothing. They are not able to own, cherish, or be thankful for the things they do possess. What they do not possess, possesses them. The envious want more and get less. The grateful are thankful for what they already have, and receive more. Do whatever you can to help your child to become a humble, grateful person.

Session Outline (51 minutes)

    I. Introduction (8 minutes)
       A. Welcome (1 minute)
       B. Review and Overview (6 minutes)
       C. Opening Prayer (1 minute)
    II. Discovery (41 minutes)
       A. Video Segment: Tantrums Needn't Be Forever (7 minutes)
       B. Kid Talk: When Kids React (5 minutes)
       C. Kid Kare: Reactive and Proactive Boundaries (10 minutes)
       D. Video Segment: I Am Happier When I Am Thankful (6 minutes)
       E. Kid Talk: Dealing with Hatred and Envy (8 minutes)
       F. Kid Kare: Giving, Limiting, and Containing (5 minutes)
   III. Wrap-up (2 minutes)

Recommended Reading

"Tantrums Needn't Be Forever: The Law of Proactivity" and "I Am Happier When I Am Thankful: The Law of Envy," chapters 10 and 11 in *Boundaries with Kids.*

Session Six

Boundary Principles Seven and Eight: The Laws of Proactivity and Envy

8 MINUTES	**INTRODUCTION**
1 minute	**Welcome**

> Call the group together and welcome the participants to Session 6: Boundary Principles Seven and Eight: The Laws of Proactivity and Envy.

6 minutes **Review and Overview**

> Participant's Guide Pages 101–2.

It's good to be back together again. I'm especially interested in hearing what you did with your kids this week. One of your Kid Kare at Home suggestions last week was to tackle a project with your children at home or in the community. Who did that—and what impact did your project have on the family dynamics, specifically on your relationship with your kids?

> Note: Be ready to share an anecdote from your own life.

Last week we looked first at the Law of Motivation and saw that healthy motivation is the desire to do the right things and to avoid the wrong ones because of empathic concern for others and because of a healthy respect for the demands of God's reality. We also looked at the Law of Evaluation, which calls us parents to make the distinction between hurt and harm, to evaluate our children's pain, and to let trials and pain that come their way teach them the lessons that build the character we will need to negotiate life.

PLANNING NOTES

_____

_____

_____

_____

_____

_____

_____

_____

_____

_____

_____

_____

_____

_____

_____

_____

_____

_____

_____

_____

_____

Session Six

Boundary Principles Seven and Eight: The Laws of Proactivity and Envy

OVERVIEW

In this session, you will

- See the value and insufficiency of reactive boundaries as you learn about the Law of Proactivity.

- Acknowledge the far greater, longer-lasting values of proactive boundaries.

- Understand that proactive boundaries encourage a child to solve problems, not just complain about them; help him define what he loves, not just what he hates; help him get out from under the control of others; and help him focus on getting his needs met, not judging the world for not being fair to him.

- Define *envy*, *entitlement*, and *gratitude* as you discuss the Law of Envy.

- Realize that, in order to give your children a balanced sense of themselves and others, you must gratify needs and some wants and frustrate others. The three skills necessary to do this are giving, limiting, and containing.

101

---

102   *Boundaries with Kids Participant's Guide*

- Recognize the importance of tolerating being hated by your children, of teaching your children to express gratitude, and of distinguishing between wishes that come from envy and wishes that are heartfelt.

→ We'll look at two more boundary principles today. The discussion of the Law of Proactivity will point out the differences and the value of each. The Law of Envy addresses envy, entitlement, and gratitude as well as calls us to gratify needs and some wants and frustrate others so that our kids develop a healthy understanding of the difference between wants and needs.

Let's open in prayer.

1 minute   ## Opening Prayer

Lord God, as we consider the work you call us parents to do—to implement such principles as the Law of Motivation and the Law of Evaluation as we raise our kids—we are so thankful that we are not in this task alone. First, we praise you, Lord, that you love our kids even more than we do. And we praise you that your Holy Spirit can work in their hearts to grow in them genuine concern about other people, a healthy respect for you and your ways, and the desire to do the right things and avoid the wrong because of that concern and respect. We praise you too that you first give us the wisdom we need to evaluate whether our children's struggles are hurtful or harmful, and then you give us peace and the privilege of prayer as we let life's trials teach them lessons and build character. Thank you that you are also here with us now as we consider two more boundary principles. Make us attentive and responsive students to what we learn today. We pray in Jesus' name. Amen.

41 MINUTES DISCOVERY

7 minutes   ## Video Segment: Tantrums Needn't Be Forever

> Remind the participants that key points of the video segment can be found on pages 103–4 of the Participant's Guide if they would like to review them at a later time.

> View Video Segment: Tantrums Needn't Be Forever

There were undoubtedly some moments in that video that reminded you of the home front. Let's spend a few minutes thinking about when your kids react.

PLANNING NOTES

_____

_____

_____

_____

_____

_____

_____

_____

_____

_____

_____

_____

_____

_____

_____

Session Six

Boundary Principles Seven and Eight: The Laws of Proactivity and Envy

OVERVIEW

In this session, you will

- See the value and insufficiency of reactive boundaries as you learn about the Law of Proactivity.
- Acknowledge the far greater, longer-lasting values of proactive boundaries.
- Understand that proactive boundaries encourage a child to solve problems, not just complain about them; help him define what he loves, not just what he hates; help him get out from under the control of others; and help him focus on getting his needs met, not judging the world for not being fair to him.
- Define *envy*, *entitlement*, and *gratitude* as you discuss the Law of Envy.
- Realize that, in order to give your children a balanced sense of themselves and others, you must gratify needs and some wants and frustrate others. The three skills necessary to do this are giving, limiting, and containing.

101

---

102   *Boundaries with Kids Participant's Guide*

- Recognize the importance of tolerating being hated by your children, of teaching your children to express gratitude, and of distinguishing between wishes that come from envy and wishes that are heartfelt.

Session Six: *Boundary Principles Seven and Eight*   103

VIDEO SEGMENT
Tantrums Needn't Be Forever

- The struggle between reactivity and proactivity, between lashing out in protest and responding maturely to problems, is a challenge in both child rearing and boundaries that exist, at some level, in all of us. It is the parent's job to help the child develop the ability to set appropriate boundaries without exploding or being impulsive.
- Children's reactive boundaries are necessary for their survival and growth. They need to be able to protest what they are against, do not like, or fear. But reactive boundaries are insufficient because children need to grow up to be defined by more than what they hate.
- Reactive boundaries signal that something needs to be dealt with; proactive boundaries fix something that is broken.
- Children who never move beyond reactive boundaries develop a victim identity. They look at most of their struggles in life as coming from the outside, not from inside themselves. Thus, they are forever prohibited from improving their lives because no problem that originates outside of us is really solvable.
- Proactive boundaries go beyond problem identification to problem solving. Your child needs to know that in protesting, she has only identified the problem, not solved it. She needs to use these feelings to motivate her to action, to address the issue at hand.
- Proactive boundaries encompass both what the child is for and against. While reactive boundaries

---

104   *Boundaries with Kids Participant's Guide*

help children identify what is "not me" and what they don't like, they also need to know what they love.

- Proactive boundaries mean others can't control the child. Children who have reactive boundaries and who live in protest are still dependent on other people. Children with proactive boundaries, however, view life, make decisions, and respond to the environment according to their own internal values and realities.
- Proactive boundaries are not about revenge and fairness but about responsibility. Reactive boundaries operate under the law "an eye for an eye." Proactive boundaries, however, are more concerned with higher motives, such as responsibility, righteousness, and love for others. Put differently, with reactive boundaries, you fight the friend who constantly bugs you. With proactive boundaries, you stop fighting and take a stand on the issue. If things do not change, you can limit your exposure to the person instead of continuing to fight.
- To summarize, proactive boundaries encourage the child to solve problems, not just complain about them; help him define what he loves, not just what he hates; get out from under the control of others; and help the child focus on getting his needs met, not judging the world for not being fair to him.

_____

_____

_____

_____

_____

_____

_____

_____

5 minutes   ## Kid Kare: When Kids React

> Participant's Guide pages 105–6.

Directions

On your own, take 5 minutes to answer the questions on page 105 of your Participant's Guide.

At this point you may think that reactive boundaries are bad for your child. The reality is, however, that they have their place in his development. Please turn to pages 107 and 109 in your Participant's Guide to learn more about that fact.

10 minutes   ## Kid Kare: Reactive and Proactive Boundaries

> Participant's Guide pages 107–9.

Directions

We will be doing this exercise in small groups of 4 or 5. You will have 10 minutes to complete this exercise. Any questions?

> Let the participants know when there is 1 minute remaining. Call the group back together after 10 minutes.

I hope this exercise has helped you learn a bit more about the movement from reactive to proactive boundaries, how to determine where your children are on that path, and how to encourage proactive boundaries in your children. Let's move on to our next video segment.

6 minutes   ## Video Segment: I Am Happier When I Am Thankful

> Remind the participants that key points of the video segment can be found on pages 110 and 111 of the Participant's Guide if they would like to review them at a later time.

> View Video Segment: I Am Happier When I Am Thankful.

The video made some important points. Let's spend some time talking about those. Please turn to page 112 in your Participant's Guide.

PLANNING NOTES

_____

_____

_____

_____

_____

_____

_____

_____

_____

_____

_____

_____

_____

_____

Session Six: *Boundary Principles Seven and Eight* 105

KID KARE
When Kids React

DIRECTIONS

On your own, take 5 minutes to answer the following questions.

1. Which of the following reactive behaviors have you seen your child adopting?

   - *Tantrums.* Your smiling, happy child turns into a screaming maniac when you, for example, say no to his desire for a toy at McDonald's. To keep the other (staring) customers from thinking you're abusing your child, you quickly purchase the toy.

   - *Oppositionalism.* Your child opposes whatever you say or ask. He defies requests to clean his room, pick up after himself, do homework, or come indoors.

   - *Whining.* Upon encountering your boundary or some other limitation, your child immediately begins complaining plaintively. There is no reasoning with her, and she can whine for hours.

   - *Impulsivity.* When denied something, your child runs away, says hurtful things, or quickly acts out in some way.

   - *Fighting and violence.* Your child's angry reactions take on physical dimensions. He is easily provoked into school fights, and he hurls objects at home.

2. Consider the following three-part description of reactivity in children:

   - Children's responses are reactions, not actions: their behavior is determined by some external influence, not by their values or thoughts.

---

106 *Boundaries with Kids Participant's Guide*

   - Children's reactions are oppositional: they take a stance against what they don't like, but not for what they desire or value.

   - Children's reactive boundaries are not value driven.

What do these facts suggest about our job description as parents? Specifically, what do these facts say about the importance of teaching our children self-control?

Session Six: *Boundary Principles Seven and Eight* 107

KID KARE
Reactive and Proactive Boundaries

DIRECTIONS

In your small group, take 10 minutes to complete this exercise.

REACTIVE BOUNDARIES

- Reactive boundaries lead to mature, loving boundaries and actions through a sequence of abilities and skills:

   1. The child is born into fear and helplessness. She is afraid of being hurt, losing love, or dying. She has little ability to care for and protect herself.

   2. The child becomes compliant out of fear. Because she fears the effects of resisting, she allows unwanted things, such as not having all her desires met, frustration, her parents' absence, even abuse.

   3. If she is loved enough to feel safe with her feelings, she begins to safely experience her rage at what she doesn't like or want.

   4. She sets her reactive boundaries and protests with tears, tantrums, or acting out.

   5. These boundaries allow her to define herself and identify the problems that need solving. She becomes free to say no as well as yes.

   6. With the support and structure of her parents, the child develops proactive boundaries, which become based on higher and higher levels of motivations, culminating in godly altruism—loving God and others. She has no need to have tantrums, as she doesn't feel helpless and controlled. She is in control of herself.

---

108 *Boundaries with Kids Participant's Guide*

   - Where are your children on this path? Put differently, where do you see each child having a potential reactive problem? What have you done to combat this? Is it working? Why or why not? What can you do differently?

PROACTIVE BOUNDARIES

Proactive boundaries go beyond problem identification to problem solving.

   - Consider a common cause of your child's tantrums. What can you say to empathize and still enforce the limits? What more appropriate expression of her feelings could you suggest if she doesn't come up with any ideas on her own? What can you do to move your child past protesting to solving the problem?

Proactive boundaries encompass both what the child is for and against.

   - What does your child feel safe protesting? What can you do to move your child toward positive values, toward taking stands for certain things? What is she learning about what she is for? What is helping that learning happen?

Session Six: *Boundary Principles Seven and Eight* 109

Proactive boundaries mean others can't control the child.

   - In what situation, if any, can you help your reactive child see that as long as he is giving up time and energy reacting, the person to whom he is reacting is in control of his precious time? What can you encourage your child to do to stop being controlled by others? What skills does he need to learn? What requirements to do that learning might you have to enforce? Also, in what ways, if any, might you be inviting your child to be dependent on you rather than learning to take responsibility for her own emotions?

Proactive boundaries are not about revenge and fairness but about responsibility.

   - When has the issue of fairness arisen in your home? In what situations do you realize you have given in to cries for fairness? Why did you do that? What is helpful about the response, "You're right—lots of things aren't fair"? Who can offer you support as you help your kids learn to cope with the fact that life isn't fair?

---

110 *Boundaries with Kids Participant's Guide*

VIDEO SEGMENT
I Am Happier When I Am Thankful

- Envy is a perpetual "wanting more." Related to envy, entitlement is when someone feels as if people owe him things or special treatment simply because he exists.

- The opposite of entitlement and envy is gratitude. Gratitude and envy have little to do with what a person actually receives. They have more to do with the character of the person. Parents must help children work through their feelings of entitlement and envy and move to a position of gratitude.

- The balance of gratification and frustration tempers the extremes of neediness and entitlement. In addition, a child learns to not see himself as a victim when he's deprived, nor does he see others as bad when they do not do what he wants. He develops a balanced view of himself and others.

- In order to give your children this balanced sense of themselves and others, you must gratify needs and some wants, and frustrate others. The three skills necessary to do this are giving, limiting, and containing.

- The parent who cannot tolerate being hated will not be able to provide the reality the child needs to overcome feeling entitled. You must be able to contain the protest, stay connected, not strike back, and remain the parent.

- Expressing gratitude is an important aspect of development. A child who is not expressing thanks is taking things for granted. Let him know that this is not appreciated by others. Help your child learn to express gratitude by setting forth your own limits in not allowing yourself to be taken for granted.

Session Six: *Boundary Principles Seven and Eight* 111

   - Determine which of your child's wishes come from envy and which are heartfelt desires. Desire moves our children (and us) to work; envy just burns within. If you don't give in to his envy, you have taught your child one of the most important lessons in life: His lack is his problem.

   - Envious people think they deserve everything, but in the end have nothing. Envy is basically pride. The envious are those who want more and get less; the grateful are those who are thankful for what they already have, and receive more. So help your child become a humble, grateful person.

8 minutes   *Kid Talk: Dealing with Hatred and Envy*

> Participant's Guide page 112.

1. How do you specifically respond to being hated? Do you react or give in? What would be a better response?

> Possible answers: Empathy: "I know, honey. It's hard." "I hate it too when I don't get to do what I want." "Life is hard, isn't it?"

2. What will you do to take care of yourself in preparation for your child's hatred? After that hatred has been expressed?

> Possible answers: Be sure to have support in your parenting efforts (spouse, friends, people with older kids).
>
> Turn to the people who support you. Turn to God and his word for reminders of his love. Review *Boundaries with Kids* for the reality check that such hatred is normal.

3. How have you handled—and now how would you like to handle—your children's desires that arise from envy?

> Possible answers: Frustration, indulgence, discussion, and prayer.
>
> Don't give in to your child's envy. Let the envious desires die and help the child achieve the ones that come from the heart. Empathize with your child's longing, help her plan to reach that goal, and encourage her.

4. Parents would do well to determine which of their child's wishes come from envy and which are heartfelt desires. What heartfelt desires—those which have stood the test of time—have your children shared with you? What did you do to support your children?

> Possible answers: Hope for a special trip, toy, bicycle, car, or sibling.
>
> Helped develop a plan for reaching the goal; prayed with her for God's guidance and provision; connected her with people who could advise or assist; encouraged during the process of working to achieve that goal.

As Dr. Townsend said in the video, "In order to give your children this balanced sense of themselves and others, you must gratify needs and some wants, and frustrate others. The three skills necessary to do

PLANNING NOTES

_____

_____

_____

_____

_____

_____

_____

_____

_____

_____

_____

KID TALK
Dealing with Hatred and Envy

1. How do you specifically respond to being hated? Do you react or give in? What would be a better response?

2. What will you do to take care of yourself in preparation for your child's hatred? After that hatred has been expressed?

3. How have you handled—and now how would you like to handle—your children's desires that arise from envy?

4. Parents would do well to determine which of their child's wishes come from envy and which are heartfelt desires. What heartfelt desires—those which have stood the test of time—have your children shared with you? What did you do to support your children?

_____

_____

_____

_____

_____

_____

_____

_____

_____

_____

_____

_____

this are giving, limiting, and containing." Let's consider now what these skills might look like in your home. Please turn to pages 113 through 116 in your Participant's Guide.

5 minutes   ### Kid Kare: Giving, Limiting, and Containing

> Participant's Guide pages 113–16.

Directions

Let's divide up into three groups. You'll have 5 minutes to begin answering the questions on giving, limiting, or containing that I assign you. I encourage you to finish the three-part exercise at home. Any questions?

> Let the participants know when there is 1 minute remaining. Call the group back together after 5 minutes.

Whether your group discussed giving, limiting, or containing, you now can undoubtedly better understand how that particular skill will help you gratify your child's needs, gratify some of his wants, and frustrate others. And doing so will enable you to teach your child that she is happier when she is thankful.

2 MINUTES   WRAP-UP

> Participant's Guide pages 117–19.

As always, there's a Kid Kare at Home section at the end of the session that will help you apply the truths that you've learned here about the Laws of Proactivity and Envy. I encourage you to read through the options and choose at least one bulleted point to wrestle with this week.

Now let's close in prayer.

Closing Prayer

Lord God, once again we have so much to think about and act on—and we're so aware of our need for you. Although we understand now the value of reactive boundaries, help us encourage our kids toward proactive boundaries, toward problem solving, good decision making, age-appropriate responsibility, and the acceptance that life is not fair. Help us also to foster an attitude of genuine gratitude in our

PLANNING NOTES

_____

_____

_____

_____

_____

_____

_____

_____

_____

_____

_____

_____

_____

KID KARE
Giving, Limiting, and Containing

DIRECTIONS

In your small group, take 5 minutes to begin answering the questions on giving, limiting, and containing that you are assigned. Finish the three-part exercise at home.

GIVING

1. *Giving* is the gratification of needs and wants. The most important gratification is the one for love, connection, and care. Each stage of childhood offers parents opportunities to give toward particular needs. At which stage is each of your children?

   - Infancy with basic needs for food, care, warmth, and safety
   - Toddlerhood with fears that need to be gratified and call for your reassurance
   - Later childhood with its needs for freedom, space, and some control and choices; with a growing ability to want what he wants and to ask for it
   - Teenage years, characterized by the desire to have things, activities, and resources (money and opportunities) to explore his skills and talents

2. What are you doing—and could you be doing—to meet your child's specific needs? Where are you giving bountifully to your children so that they can be healthily weaned for life?

LIMITING

1. The concept of *limiting* is making sure children do not get too much or do not get inappropriate things; that their wish to be in control of everything is not gratified. In addition, limiting is disciplining and managing a child's choices and consequences. At what stage below is your child? Considering your child's age, how well are you doing with setting and enforcing limits?

   - Infancy: She is limited by physical existence, yet learning that she has had all she needs and now just has to go to sleep.
   - Toddlerhood: The word *no* has meaning; the child is learning that he is not entitled to everything he wants, that he is not in control, and that he must use words and not whine or manipulate to get what he needs.
   - Later childhood: When a child wants toys he can't have, he learns that the world isn't going to just give him what he wants—he has to earn what he wants. He learns that he won't get something simply because a friend or sibling has it—life is not fair if defined as "equal."
   - Teenage years: Teens need more and more freedom and choices and opportunities to be responsible, but they also need clear and enforced limits to obey, all this in preparation for taking on the guardian and manager role for themselves.

2. Throughout the developmental spectrum, limiting your children is important in overcoming envy and entitlement. Read the statements about limits. Which statements about the importance of limits are especially significant to you? In light of what these statements say, why are limits a crucial way for you to love your child and meet her greatest needs?

Here are some thoughts on the role of limiting:

- Limits begin in infancy when, having had all their needs met, infants experience separateness at times.
- Limits begin to kick in formally in toddlerhood as children learn they are not the boss, and limits continue throughout the teen years.
- Limits teach children that they are not entitled to whatever they want, even though their wants may be good. They have to work to achieve what they want; desire is not enough.
- Limits teach children that life is not fair, if they define fair as equal. They will never have the same as everyone else. Some will have more, some will have less than they will.
- Limits help children learn that their feelings are not ultimate reality.
- Limits are important in bringing out children's protest so parents can empathize with their children and contain their feelings while keeping the limit.
- Limits and discipline show children their badness, so they do not think they are innocent victims of the universe.
- Limits instill confidence because children find they can survive the deprivation of some of their wants and learn to meet some of their own needs.
- Limits give them a structure for how to treat others. Children who have experienced loving limits can set them.
- Limits help them experience grieving for what they cannot control, so they can let it go and resolve it.

CONTAINING

1. *Containing* consists of helping a child to work through her feelings about a limit and to internalize that limit as character. Containing is, then, the addition of love, understanding, and structure to limits. As children learn limits and begin to realize

---

they are not in control, it is typical for them to respond with anger. What dangerous message do you communicate, though, if you remove the limit because of that protest?

2. When a limit stays, your child may become enraged, and someone must turn that rage into sadness, grief, and resolution. You do this with comfort, care, connection, and empathy.

   - "I know, honey, it's hard."
   - "I agree. It's not fair."
   - "I hate it too when I don't get to do what I want."
   - "I understand. No, you still can't go."
   - "Livin's hard, huh?"

What important message do you communicate to a child who has bumped up against an immovable limit when you use these statements?

Closing Prayer

Lord God, once again I have so much to think about and act on—and I'm so aware of my need for you. Although I understand now the value of reactive boundaries, help me encourage my kids toward proactive boundaries, toward problem solving, good decision making, age-appropriate responsibility, and the acceptance that life is not fair. Help me also to foster an attitude of genuine gratitude in my kids—and, Lord, may you enable me to model that. I ask for your strength so I can tolerate being hated and your wisdom so that I can discern between envy and heartfelt desire. Help me help my kids become humble, grateful people. Help me to be such a person too. I pray in Jesus' name—and with genuine gratitude for the gift of salvation that is available through him. Amen.

Kid Kare at Home

1. Finish any exercises you started in class and did not have a chance to complete.

The Law of Proactivity

2. What boundary issues can you anticipate having to deal with in the next week or so? Review the skills described below and then thoughtfully plan how you will use that particular skill in a teachable moment.

   - *Pausing instead of reacting.* When your child reacts instantly in protest, make him repeat the desired action several times, talking him through it each time,

---

until he sees he doesn't have to react. The child who angrily slams the door must see that he is capable of twenty or thirty soft closes, even when he is mad.

- *Observation of himself.* Help your child become a student of himself. Go over the incident, helping him see other realities besides his frustration.
- *Perspective on her feelings as well as other people's feelings.* Give your child your input on her anger and rage. Remind her that while she may think her feelings are absolute truth, feelings don't always show us absolute reality. Help her look at her feelings as feelings—they will go away. Remind her that others' feelings are important too.
- *Problem solving.* Help your child see other alternatives to solving his problem or getting his need met: "If Bobby won't play with you, how about trying Billy?"
- *Reality that calls for negotiation and compromise.* Help your child compromise and negotiate results that aren't black and white. It is important for her to learn that her needs won't be met perfectly, but that good enough is good enough. She may not have the lead in the school play, for example, but her part is a good part.
- *Initiative to be proactive to solve or avoid the problem.* Your child must understand that until she is proactive with the problem, she will be forever reacting to the same problem, with no solution. Don't reinforce the griping, push her to be a solver.
- *Other people.* If you have done your best and you don't know what to do, ask someone you trust.

The Law of Envy

If you have good limits and boundaries, you will empathize with your child's longing, help him to plan to reach the goal, and encourage him. If you don't give in to his envy, you have taught him one of the most important lessons in life—that his lack is his problem.

3. When have you seen your child look at the world outside himself, see things he wants, and be motivated by a desire to work?

4. Is your child looking at his abilities, his possessions, or his skills, and feeling sad at what's missing? Put differently, where are you giving in to or getting stuck with a problem of your child's envy? What will you do differently in order to be more effective?

5. Don't be a Lone Ranger Mom or Dad. Whom can or do you go to for solid parenting advice? Make the phone call this week!

BETWEEN SESSIONS READING

"Tantrums Needn't Be Forever: The Law of Proactivity" and "I Am Happier When I Am Thankful: The Law of Envy," chapters 10 and 11 in *Boundaries with Kids*.

kids—and, Lord, may you enable us to model that. We ask for your strength so we can tolerate being hated and your wisdom so that we can discern between envy and heartfelt desire. Help us help our kids become humble, grateful people. Help each one of us to be such a person too. We pray in Jesus' name—and with genuine gratitude for the gift of salvation that is available through him. Amen.

PLANNING NOTES

_____

_____

_____

_____

_____

_____

_____

_____

_____

_____

Session Six: *Boundary Principles Seven and Eight* 117

Closing Prayer

Lord God, once again I have so much to think about and act on—and I'm so aware of my need for you. Although I understand now the value of reactive boundaries, help me encourage my kids toward proactive boundaries, toward problem solving, good decision making, age-appropriate responsibility, and the acceptance that life is not fair. Help me also to foster an attitude of genuine gratitude in my kids—and, Lord, may you enable me to model that. I ask for your strength so I can tolerate being hated and your wisdom so that I can discern between envy and heartfelt desire. Help me help my kids become humble, grateful people. Help me to be such a person too. I pray in Jesus' name—and with genuine gratitude for the gift of salvation that is available through him. Amen.

Kid Kare at Home

1. Finish any exercises you started in class and did not have a chance to complete.

The Law of Proactivity

2. What boundary issues can you anticipate having to deal with in the next week or so? Review the skills described below and then thoughtfully plan how you will use that particular skill in a teachable moment.

- *Pausing instead of reacting.* When your child reacts instantly in protest, make him repeat the desired action several times, talking him through it each time,

---

_____

_____

_____

_____

_____

_____

_____

_____

_____

_____

_____

_____

Session Seven

Boundary Principles Nine and Ten: The Laws of Activity and Exposure

BEFORE YOU LEAD

Key Points

- **The Law of Activity**—One of the greatest gifts you can give your child is to help build in her a tendency toward activity. A child must understand that the solution to her problems and the answer to her needs always begins not with someone else but with her.

- *Do not confuse dependency with passivity.* We are designed to be actively dependent on God and others all our lives. *By the same token, do not confuse activity with self-sufficiency.* Active people don't attempt to do everything on their own.

- Kids struggle with passivity due to fear, an inability to structure goals, clairvoyant expectations, conflicted aggression, laziness, an entitled attitude, an underlying emotional disorder, or drug and alcohol problems.

- Six guidelines can help your children be seekers and growers.

- Your child needs you to be the loving, limiting, provoking agent who teases out his active parts. Just as the mother bird knows when to push the baby bird out of the nest, use your experience, judgment, and the help of God and others to enable your child to take initiative to own his life.

- **The Law of Exposure**—One of the most important principles in relationship is direct communication and full disclosure of whatever is going on in the relationship.

- Many people do not communicate directly. Instead, they practice avoidance (ignoring the person or the problem) or triangulation (bringing in a third person) or overlooking.

117

- The Law of Exposure says that life is better lived in the light— that is, things are better out in the open even if these things are negative.

- Six principles can help your children to be open and honest in their relationships.

- The ultimate boundary is love, and everything is ultimately about relationship. Relationship heals, comforts, and structures our experience.

- As Jesus said, all of the boundaries in the world can be summed up in these two laws: "Love God" and "Love your neighbor as yourself."

Synopsis

The Law of Activity—One of the greatest gifts you can give your child is to help build in her a tendency toward activity. A child must understand that the solution to her problems and the answer to her needs always begins not with someone else but with her. *Do not confuse dependency with passivity.* We are designed to be actively dependent on God and others all our lives. *By the same token, do not confuse activity with self-sufficiency.* Active people don't attempt to do everything on their own.

Passivity is the opposite of activity and initiative, and kids struggle with passivity for such reasons as fear, an inability to structure goals, clairvoyant expectations, conflicted aggression, laziness, an entitled attitude, and sometimes an underlying emotional disorder or drug and alcohol problems.

The following six guidelines can help your children be seekers and growers.

1. Become an active person, not just a parent.

2. Work through any enabling of your child's passivity.

3. Require initiative and problem solving.

4. Teach your child to move toward relationship.

5. Make passivity more painful than activity.

6. Allow time for the process to develop.

Generally, there comes a point when, if the process is working right, your child's activity level will increase. Your child needs you to be the loving, limiting, provoking agent who teases out his active parts. Just as the mother bird knows when to push the baby bird out of the nest, use your experience, judgment, and the help of God and others to help your child take initiative to own his life.

The Law of Exposure—One of the most important principles in relationship is direct communication and full disclosure of whatever is going on in the relationship. But many people do not communicate directly. Instead, they practice avoidance (ignoring the person or the problem) or triangulation (bringing in a third person) or overlooking. The Law of Exposure says that life is better lived in the light—that is, things are better out in the open even if these things are negative.

Open communication does not mean that we bring up every slight thing that bothers us. But where values are violated or someone is injured or behaving unacceptably, then overlooking, avoiding, or triangulating causes more problems in a relationship. The following six principles will help your children to be open and honest in their relationships.

Rule #1: Live the Law of Exposure Yourself.
Rule #2: Make the Boundaries Clear.
Rule #3: Cure Their Fears and Make Communication Safe.
Rule #4: Don't Reinforce Non-Expression.
Rule #5: Don't Get in the Middle.
Rule #6: Teach Them Boundary Words to Use.

The ultimate boundary is love, and everything is ultimately about relationship. As Jesus said, all of the boundaries in the world can be summed up in these two laws: "Love God" and "Love your neighbor as yourself." Relationship heals, comforts, and structures our experience. So, as you work on being the kind of person to whom your children can take their feelings, fears, thoughts, desires, and experiences, require them to love God and love others. And they will be much less afraid of both their experiences and love itself.

Session Outline (51 minutes)

    I. Introduction (8 minutes)
        A. Welcome (1 minute)
        B. Review and Overview (6 minutes)
        C. Opening Prayer (1 minute)
    II. Discovery (43 minutes)
        A. Video Segment: Jump-starting My Engine (7 minutes)
        B. Kid Talk: From Passive to Active (8 minutes)
        C. Kid Kare: What Can You Do about a Passive Child? (5 minutes)
        D. Video Segment: Honesty Is the Best Policy (5 minutes)
        E. Kid Talk: Bring It to Relationship (10 minutes)
        F. Kid Kare: Principles for Openness and Honesty (8 minutes)
    III. Wrap-up (2 minutes)

RECOMMENDED READING

"Jump-starting My Engine: The Law of Activity" and "Honesty Is the Best Policy: The Law of Exposure," chapters 12 and 13 in *Boundaries with Kids*.

Session Seven

Boundary Principles Nine and Ten: The Laws of Activity and Exposure

10 MINUTES   INTRODUCTION

1 minute   Welcome

> Call the group together.

Welcome back! Today we'll tackle the final two boundary principles, but before we do that, I want to ask you about the two we discussed last week.

8 minutes   Review and Overview

> Participant's Guide page 121.

Kid Kare at Home encouraged you to teach any of seven important skills about the Law of Proactivity if and when the opportunity arose. Can anyone remind us of one or more of these skills?

> The seven skills are
> 1. *Pausing instead of reacting*—When your child reacts instantly in protest, make him repeat the desired action several times, talking him through it each time, until he sees he doesn't have to react.
> 2. *Observation of himself*—Help your child see other realities besides his frustration.
> 3. *Perspective on her feelings as well as other people's feelings*—Help your child look at her feelings as feelings: They will go away. They don't always show us absolute reality. Others' feelings are important too.

120

PLANNING NOTES

_____

_____

_____

_____

_____

_____

_____

_____

_____

_____

_____

Session Seven

Boundary Principles Nine and Ten: The Laws of Activity and Exposure

OVERVIEW

In this session, you will

- Learn the Law of Activity and the importance of activity in the development of boundaries.

- Identify seven reasons why kids struggle with passivity.

- Discover six guidelines for helping your children be seekers and growers.

- Be reminded of the importance of direct communication and full disclosure of whatever is going on in the relationship as you discuss the Law of Exposure.

- Be cautioned to avoid indirect communication like avoidance (ignoring the person or the problem), triangulation (bringing in a third person), or overlooking.

- Explore six principles that will help your children to be open and honest in their relationships.

121

_____

_____

_____

_____

_____

_____

_____

_____

_____

_____

_____

_____

_____

4. *Problem solving*—Help your child see other alternatives to solving his problem or getting his need met.
5. *Reality that calls for negotiation and compromise*—Help your child compromise and negotiate results that aren't black and white.
6. *Initiative to be proactive to solve or avoid the problem*—Your child must understand that until she is proactive with the problem, she will be forever reacting to the same problem, with no solution.
7. *Other people*—If you have done your best and you don't know what to do, ask someone you trust.

Which of you worked on one of these skills this week? We'd like to hear about it and learn from your experience.

Note: Be ready to share an anecdote from your own life for this and the following two questions.

We also talked about the Law of Envy.

When, if at all, this week did you notice your child look at his abilities, his possessions, or his skills, feel sad at what's missing, and be moved to work on improving his feeling of contentment?

What did you do to help your child become a humble, grateful person?

Today we're going to be discussing our final two boundary principles: the Law of Activity and the Law of Exposure. We will identify seven reasons why kids struggle with passivity and discover six guidelines for helping our children be seekers and growers. We will also discuss direct and indirect communication and explore six principles that will help our children to be open and honest in their relationships.

Before we begin, let's open with a word of prayer.

1 minute   *Opening Prayer*

Lord God, all these boundary principles can seem overwhelming and the task of parenting so huge. Thank you that we can turn to you for guidance, strength, and insight. Help us to be students of our children so that we can know what to work on and when. Keep us faithfully praying for them because the work of your Holy Spirit can do far more than our most passionate words. We ask you to be with us now. Teach us, heavenly Father, how to be better parents to the children you've entrusted to our care. We pray in Jesus' name. Amen.

PLANNING NOTES

_____

_____

_____

_____

_____

_____

_____

_____

_____

_____

_____

Session Seven

Boundary Principles Nine and Ten: The Laws of Activity and Exposure

OVERVIEW

In this session, you will

- Learn the Law of Activity and the importance of activity in the development of boundaries.
- Identify seven reasons why kids struggle with passivity.
- Discover six guidelines for helping your children be seekers and growers.
- Be reminded of the importance of direct communication and full disclosure of whatever is going on in the relationship as you discuss the Law of Exposure.
- Be cautioned to avoid indirect communication like avoidance (ignoring the person or the problem), triangulation (bringing in a third person), or overlooking.
- Explore six principles that will help your children to be open and honest in their relationships.

121

_____

_____

_____

_____

_____

_____

_____

_____

_____

_____

_____

_____

_____

_____

43 MINUTES DISCOVERY

7 minutes   ## *Video Segment: Jump-starting My Engine*

Now let's look at our last two boundary principles. The first one is the Law of Activity.

> Remind the participants that key points of the video segment can be found on pages 122–23 of the Participant's Guide if they would like to review them at a later time.

> View Video Segment: Jump-starting My Engine

As Dr. Cloud said, one of the greatest gifts we can give our children is to help build in each of them a tendency toward activity. That being the case, let's take a few minutes to consider how passive our kids are and what we want to do in response to their resistance when we encourage them to be active. Keep in mind that some of the behavior we'll be talking about is normal in the process of growing up and maturing. But if there is a pattern of these behaviors and dynamics, don't ignore it. Take appropriate action with your child.

8 minutes   ## *Kid Kare: From Passive to Active*

> Participant's Guide pages 124–25.

Directions

Divide into groups of four. You will have 7 minutes to discuss the questions that appear on pages 124 and 125. Any questions?

> Let the participants know when there is 1 minute remaining. Call the group back together after 7 minutes.

However passive or active your children are, you—and they—can benefit from the suggestions you'll find in our next exercise: What Can You Do about a Passive Child? Please turn to pages 126 through 129 in your Participant's Guide.

PLANNING NOTES

_____

_____

_____

_____

_____

_____

_____

_____

_____

_____

_____

_____

_____

---

122   *Boundaries with Kids Participant's Guide*

VIDEO SEGMENT
Jump-starting My Engine

- One of the greatest gifts you can give your child is to help build in her a tendency toward activity. A child must understand that the solution to her problems and the answer to her needs always begins not with someone else but with her.
- *Do not confuse dependency with passivity.* We are designed to be actively dependent on God and others all our lives.
- *By the same token, do not confuse activity with self-sufficiency.* Active people don't attempt to do everything on their own.
- Kids struggle with passivity for several reasons. First, **fear** may be at the root of passivity—fear of closeness, of conflict, of failure.
- Passivity can result from **an inability to structure goals.** Some kids sink into passive stances because they have problems thinking through what steps to take to get what they want.
- **Clairvoyant expectations** are another reason for passivity. A child may feel he shouldn't have to ask for what he needs, on the assumption that you should know before he asks.
- A fourth root of passivity is **conflicted aggression.** Some kids are not innately passive. They are aggressive in some areas and nonresponsive in others.
- Not surprisingly, **laziness** can be the reason for passivity.
- A major cause of passivity in children is **an entitled attitude,** a demand for special treatment.

Session Seven: Boundary Principles Nine and Ten   **123**

- Sometimes childhood passivity can be a symptom of an underlying emotional disorder or of drug and alcohol problems.
- Here are six guidelines for helping your children be seekers and growers.
  1. Become an active person, not just a parent.
  2. Work through any enabling of your child's passivity.
  3. Require initiative and problem solving.
  4. Teach your child to move toward relationship.
  5. Make passivity more painful than activity.
  6. Allow time for the process to develop.
- Just as the mother bird knows when to push the baby bird out of the nest, use your experience, judgment, and the help of God and others to help your child take initiative to own his life.

---

124   *Boundaries with Kids Participant's Guide*

KID KARE
From Passive to Active

DIRECTIONS

Divide into groups of four. You will have 7 minutes to discuss the questions below.

Children exhibit passivity in a variety of ways, among them:
- *Procrastination:* Your child responds to you at the last possible moment. He takes an enormous amount of time doing what he doesn't want to do and very little time doing what he wants to do.
- *Ignoring:* Your child shuts out your instruction, either pretending not to hear you or simply disregarding you.
- *Lack of initiative:* Your child avoids new experiences, and stays in familiar activities and patterns.
- *Living in a fantasy world:* Your child tends to be more inward-oriented than invested in the real world. He seems happier when he's lost in his head.
- *Passive defiance:* The child resists your requests by looking blankly or sullenly at you, then simply doing nothing. She shows her anger and contempt toward your authority without words.
- *Isolation:* Your child avoids contact with others, preferring to stay in her room. Rather than confront, argue, or fight with you, she walks away when you present a problem.

1. What evidence of any of these passive behaviors have you noticed in your child(ren)? Be specific—and be open to members of your small group suggesting that what you're seeing is indeed normal in the process of growing up and maturing.

Session Seven: Boundary Principles Nine and Ten   **125**

2. When have you seen your kid actively rise to a challenge or tackle something new rather than procrastinating, ignoring your instructions, staying in a familiar pattern, living in a fantasy world, being passively defiant, or isolating himself?

3. In what current situation is your child choosing to be passive rather than active? What might you do to promote activity on his part? Who will support you during the protest and perhaps even the anger that will most likely ensue?

_____

_____

_____

_____

_____

_____

_____

5 minutes   ### Kid Kare: What Can You Do about a Passive Child?

Directions

Alone or with your spouse, take the next 5 minutes to begin working through these action steps. You can finish up the exercise later this week. Any questions?

> Let the participants know when there is 1 minute remaining. Call the group back together after 5 minutes.

The doctors' mother bird analogy is very helpful. We need to know when to push the baby bird out of the nest so our kids will learn to take initiative in their lives. We also need to teach them that "honesty is the best policy" for life, and that's the name of our next video. You'll find notes on pages 131 and 132 of your Participant's Guide.

5 minutes   ## Video Segment: Honesty Is the Best Policy

> Remind the participants that key points of the video segment can be found on pages 130–31 of the Participant's Guide if they would like to review them at a later time.

> View Video Segment: Honesty Is the Best Policy.

As we just heard in the video, the Law of Exposure says that life is better lived in the light—that is, things are better out in the open even if these things are negative.

Please turn to page 132 of your Participant's Guide.

10 minutes   ## Kid Talk: Bring It to Relationship

> Participant's Guide page 132.

1. As Dr. Townsend just said, everything is ultimately about relationship. Jesus taught that all of the "boundaries" in the world can be summed up in two laws: "Love God" and "Love your neighbor as yourself." Why is the use of boundary words one way of loving your neighbor as yourself?

PLANNING NOTES

_____

_____

_____

_____

_____

_____

_____

_____

_____

_____

_____

_____

_____

---

126   *Boundaries with Kids Participant's Guide*

KID KARE
What Can You Do about a Passive Child?

DIRECTIONS

Alone or with your spouse, take the next 5 minutes to begin working through these action steps. However passive or active your children are, you—and they—can still benefit from the suggestions you'll find.

• *Become an active person, not just a parent.* A child must internalize a model of someone who has a life of her own.

1. What are you doing—or could you be doing—to let your child know you have interests and relationships that don't involve her? What trips do you take and activities do you do without her?

2. What are you doing to show her that you take active responsibility in meeting your own needs and solving your own problems?

• *Work through any enabling of your child's passivity.* Don't confuse your love with rescuing your child from himself.

1. Whom will you ask this week about whether you are stretching your child's growth muscles sufficiently?

2. Are you avoiding setting limits in the academic, work, social, spiritual, and behavioral areas of your child's life? Are you afraid of discussing these problems

---

Session Seven: *Boundary Principles Nine and Ten*   127

because of possible conflict? Is your home a retreat from responsibility, or a place of movement and growth? What do your answers suggest about what changes you could make? Be specific—and start working on one of these changes this week.

• *Require initiative and problem solving.* Your child's tendency is to let you do all the work. It is your fault if you do it.

1. In what situations that you can expect to encounter this week could you say, "I'm sorry, but that's your responsibility. I hope you solve your problem; it sounds difficult, but I'm pulling for you"?

2. What kind of response to "That's your responsibility . . ." do you expect? What will you do to show empathy yet hold the limit?

• *Teach your child to move toward relationship.* Passive children often avoid relationships, which are some of the good resources God designed to help them live life.

1. What will you do or say to help your child see that relationship is the source of comfort in emotional pain, feeling loved inside, fuel for being assertive and being sustained through life, information for solving problems, and structure for growth? What are you modeling about these valuable aspects of relationship?

---

128   *Boundaries with Kids Participant's Guide*

2. With which of your kids, if any, might you have the opportunity to say, "Sounds like you're having trouble, but I will wait to help you until you ask"? How will you respond when the request finally comes?

• *Make passivity more painful than activity.* Don't let your child be comfortable in a passive role. He risks getting lost in the shuffle.

1. What will you say some time this week to let your child know that you prefer active mistakes to passivity?

2. A child who tries to set the table and spills everything receives praise and rewards. When he avoids the task, he loses dessert that night. What will you do to make passivity more painful than activity for your child? Set up some consequences for situations where you can expect him to be more passive than you want him to be—and then put your plan into action.

• *Allow time for the process to develop.* Kids who struggle with passivity have spent much of their lives fearing and avoiding risk, failure, and pain. So don't expect your child to be a problem-solving dynamo overnight.

Session Seven: *Boundary Principles Nine and Ten*   129

1. What will you do to reward little moves this week?

2. And what little moves can you be on the lookout for?

---

130   *Boundaries with Kids Participant's Guide*

VIDEO SEGMENT
Honesty Is the Best Policy

THE LAW OF EXPOSURE

• One of the most important principles in relationship is direct communication and full disclosure of whatever is going on in the relationship.

• Many people do not communicate directly. Instead, they practice avoidance (ignoring the person or the problem) or triangulation (bringing in a third person) or overlooking.

• The Law of Exposure says that life is better lived in the light—that is, things are better out in the open even if these things are negative.

• Open communication does not mean that we bring up every slight thing or everything that bothers us. But where values are violated or someone is injured or behaving unacceptably, then overlooking, avoiding, or triangulating causes more problems in a relationship.

• The following six principles will help your children be open and honest in their relationships.

Rule #1: Live the Law of Exposure Yourself

Rule #2: Make the Boundaries Clear

Rule #3: Cure Their Fears and Make Communication Safe

Rule #4: Don't Reinforce Non-Expression

Rule #5: Don't Get in the Middle

Rule #6: Teach Them Boundary Words to Use

Session Seven: *Boundary Principles Nine and Ten*   131

• The ultimate boundary is love, and everything is ultimately about relationship.

• All of the boundaries in the world can be summed up in these two laws that Jesus said: "Love God" and "Love your neighbor as yourself."

---

132   *Boundaries with Kids Participant's Guide*

KID TALK
Bring It to Relationship

1. As Dr. Townsend just said, everything is ultimately about relationship. And Jesus taught that all of the "boundaries" in the world can be summed up in two laws: "Love God" and "Love your neighbor as yourself." Why is the use of boundary words one way of loving your neighbor as yourself?

2. Relationship heals, comforts, and structures our experience. Think about the people you turn to for healing, comfort, and structure. What specific things do those people offer you?

3. Now think about the relationships that have helped you learn that the love we need is bigger than what we are feeling. What made those relationships helpful?

4. What can you do to be the kind of parent to whom your children can take their feelings, fears, thoughts, desires, and experiences?

> Possible answers: We are honoring our relationship by being honest. We are giving them permission to be honest and say no to us. When we say no, we may be keeping people from hurting us just as we would want to avoid hurting them.

2. Relationship heals, comforts, and structures our experience. Think about the people you turn to for healing, comfort, and structure. What specific things do those people offer you?

> Possible answers: Compassion; listening as opposed to problem solving; prayer; advice when I ask; perspective; the freedom to think out loud without being judged.

3. Now think about the relationships that have helped you learn that the love we need is bigger than what we are feeling. What made those relationships helpful?

> Possible answers: Being loved made the current very real, very big problem seem less important. Being loved pointed me to God's love. Being loved offered comfort and hope. Being loved reminded me that relationship is more important than circumstances, however difficult they are.

4. What can you do to be the kind of parent to whom your children can take their feelings, fears, thoughts, desires, and experiences?

> Possible answers: Listen better. Learn to keep my mouth shut when I want to give advice, solve the problem, lecture, or gasp. Share appropriately some of my own fears, feelings, dreams, and experiences.

As Dr. Cloud and Dr. Townsend have helped us see, everything is ultimately about relationship, and relationship heals, comforts, and structures our experiences. The lifeblood of such healthy relationships is open, honest communication. So, no matter how open our kids are, we can all benefit from a review of some principles for safe and healthy communication. Please turn to pages 133 through 136 in your Participant's Guide.

8 minutes   ## Kid Kare: Principles for Openness and Honesty

> Participant's Guide pages 133–36.

PLANNING NOTES

_____

_____

_____

_____

_____

_____

_____

_____

_____

_____

_____

_____

_____

_____

_____

_____

_____

_____

_____

KID TALK
Bring It to Relationship

1. As Dr. Townsend just said, everything is ultimately about relationship. And Jesus taught that all of the "boundaries" in the world can be summed up in two laws: "Love God" and "Love your neighbor as yourself." Why is the use of boundary words one way of loving your neighbor as yourself?

2. Relationship heals, comforts, and structures our experience. Think about the people you turn to for healing, comfort, and structure. What specific things do those people offer you?

3. Now think about the relationships that have helped you learn that the love we need is bigger than what we are feeling. What made those relationships helpful?

4. What can you do to be the kind of parent to whom your children can take their feelings, fears, thoughts, desires, and experiences?

KID KARE
Principles for Openness and Honesty

DIRECTIONS

Alone or with your spouse, take the next 8 minutes to start the following exercise.

Rule #1: Live the Law of Exposure Yourself

Remember Gary's mom? She would not ask people directly for what she wanted, and she would not tell them what they had done wrong.

1. Consider what you are modeling in your home. Do you ask people, especially your spouse, for what you want? Do you tell people what they have done wrong or what they have done to irritate you? What—good or bad—are you teaching your kids by your behavior?

2. About what current situation with your children would it be wise for you to communicate directly?

Rule #2: Make the Boundaries Clear

When you have expectations and rules for your children, make sure they know them.

1. What rules in your home do you want to be part of your children's internal structure? List your top five.

---

2. What are you doing—or will you do—to make sure your children know these rules? Are these boundaries clear to your children? If you're not sure, ask them!

Rule #3: Cure Their Fears and Make Communication Safe

1. What is your typical response to each of the following situations?
   - Your child is angry at a limit.

   - Your child is upset with something you did wrong to her.

   - Your child is hurt by life.

2. In each situation, are you pulling away from your child or staying connected? Are you therefore reinforcing her fears of loss of love or reprisal—or are you curing them?

3. How do you want to respond to your child this week when she is angry at a limit, upset with something you did wrong to her, or hurt by life?

Rule #4: Don't Reinforce Non-Expression

Generally, withdrawn and defiant children are afraid. Staying soft and loving, but at the same time not giving in to their non-expression will let them know that you are on the side of their fear and pain, but not on the side of their way of handling it.

1. To what degree and when is non-expression an issue with your child? Is "Use your words" effective?

2. You may have to be more active about pursuing your child's feelings. Interpreting the silence or asking questions helps: "It seems like you are mad/sad right now"; "I think you might be upset with me." What do you do—or can you do—to show affection even as you require communication?

3. Does your child ever communicate with actions, such as tantrums, yelling, name calling, and running away? What do you do—or will you start doing this week—to disallow this form of expression and encourage verbal communication?

Rule #5: Don't Get in the Middle

In general, except when the situation is unsafe, children need to work out their own conflicts.

1. What will you say the next time one of your children tattles on another, trying to put you in the middle? What might you do to keep the conflict between them so they learn important conflict resolution skills?

---

2. This same principle applies to the other parent, to friends, and even to other authorities in your child's life. What current or recurring situation will give you the chance to encourage your child to work out a conflict on her own? What will you do to empathize yet stay out of the middle?

Rule #6: Teach Them Boundary Words to Use

Which one or two of the following statements might your child find especially helpful right now? What role-plays will you do to give your child practice saying—and hearing himself say—these important boundary words?
- "No."
- "No, I don't feel comfortable with that."
- "No, I don't want to."
- "No, I won't do that."
- "No, my parents don't allow that."
- "No, God does not want me to do that."
- "No, I learned that we don't touch each other's private places."
- "No, I don't like drugs. They kill people."

Directions

Alone or with your spouse, take the next 8 minutes to start the following exercise. Any questions?

> Let the participants know when there is 1 minute remaining. Call the group back together after 8 minutes.

Honesty takes work and it often means taking risks, but honesty really is the best policy. And our God, who is Light and Truth, will enable you and me to do the important work of being honest.

Please turn to pages 137 through 144 in your Participant's Guide.

2 MINUTES   WRAP-UP

Your Kid Kare at Home this week gives you a chance to work a little bit more on the Law of Passivity and the Law of Exposure. You'll also be encouraged to review all ten boundary principles we've been working on because next week, at our last meeting, Dr. Cloud and Dr. Townsend will be giving us Six Steps to Implementing Boundaries with Your Kids. Let's close in prayer.

Closing Prayer

Lord God, the ideas we've heard about and discussed today make so much sense! Now we ask you to help us apply them and live them out in our families. And we know that these good traits must start with us, so we are praying for ourselves even as we pray for our children.

Show us, heavenly Father, how to build in our kids a tendency toward activity. Make us as well as our kids seekers and growers, people who try, fail, learn, and try again. Show us where, if at all, we are enabling passivity in our kids and where we can require initiative and problem solving. May we know as mother birds know when to push the baby out of the nest.

And, Lord, grow us in those areas where we need growth so that we can help our kids learn early on the value of direct communication. Teach us safe and loving communication and the proper use of boundary words so that we might teach our children. Help us as a family and as individuals to live in the light, to be open even about negative things. We ask these things in Jesus' name. Amen.

PLANNING NOTES

_____

_____

_____

_____

_____

_____

_____

Session Seven: *Boundary Principles Nine and Ten* 137

Closing Prayer

Lord God, the ideas I heard about today make so much sense! Now I ask you to help me apply them and live them out in my family. And I know that these good traits must start with me, so I am praying for myself even as I pray for my children.

Show me, heavenly Father, how to build in my kids a tendency toward activity. Make me as well as each of my children a seeker and grower, a person who tries, fails, learns, and tries again. Show me both where, if at all, I am enabling passivity in my kids and where I can require initiative and problem solving. May I know as mother birds know when to push the baby out of the nest.

And, Lord, grow me in those areas where I can grow so that I can help my kids learn early on the value of direct communication. Teach me safe and loving communication and the proper use of boundary words so that I might teach my children. Help my family and help me as an individual to live in the light, to be open even about negative things. I ask these things in Jesus' name. Amen.

Kid Kare at Home

- Finish any exercises you started in class and did not have a chance to complete.

The Law of Activity

If you have determined that your kid is more passive than active (passive behaviors are listed on page 126), try requiring initiative and problem solving by saying, "I'm sorry, but that's your responsibility. I hope you solve your problem. It sounds difficult, but I'm pulling for you." Or you might have the occasion to encourage your child to

---

138 *Boundaries with Kids Participant's Guide*

move toward relationship by saying, "Sounds like you're having trouble, but I'll wait to help you until you ask." Also, wherever your child falls on the spectrum between active and passive, read through the corresponding questions below. If your child is more passive than active, come up with a specific step you can take this week to encourage activity.

Fear

Your children may be nonresponsive because of underlying fears or anxieties that paralyze them from taking initiative. Overwhelming fear causes children to take a protective and defensive stance toward the challenges of life.

- *Closeness*—Some children are afraid of being close and vulnerable with others. What are you doing—or could you be doing—to make school, church, sports, arts, and other social activities a normal and expected part of family life? What do you do to support your child before and after he enters a social situation?

- *Conflict*—Some kids are actively involved when everything is going okay, but become afraid and passive around anger or conflict. What are you doing—or could you be doing—to normalize conflict and pain, to teach your child that conflict is okay and that she will survive it? What are you modeling in this regard?

- *Failure*—Afraid of making a mistake, kids often avoid taking initiative and thereby reduce the chance

---

Session Seven: *Boundary Principles Nine and Ten* 139

that they will fail. What are you doing—or could you be doing—to normalize failure for your children? What stories of your failures are they aware of? When, if ever, have they seen you fail and laugh at yourself?

Inability to Structure Goals

Some kids sink into passive stances because they have problems thinking through what steps to take to get what they want. Their tolerance for frustration is also generally low.

- What evidence have you seen that your child can think through steps for getting from point A to point B?

- What chores that have some complexity (cooking, cleaning, grocery shopping, yard maintenance, even home repairs) could you give your child to help him develop confidence in his ability to perform? Give your child one this week.

Clairvoyant Expectations

A child may feel he shouldn't have to ask for what he needs, on the assumption that you should know before he asks. As children grow up, they must let their needs be known clearly.

- How easily does your child communicate his needs? When, for instance, has he gotten upset because you

---

140 *Boundaries with Kids Participant's Guide*

didn't ask the right questions, you forgot something he wanted, or you didn't understand why he was unhappy?

- What does your child see in you about how to make needs known?

- Look for a situation in which you can explain, "Even though I love you very much, I can't read your mind. If you don't use your words and say what you want, you will not get a response." What else will you do to let your child know you really want to help him meet his needs and solve his problems?

Conflicted Aggression

Some kids are not innately passive. They are aggressive in some areas and nonresponsive in others. These kids have the necessary active, assertive ingredients, but they have difficulty accessing them in certain areas.

- In what areas of life (functional, relational, some functional, some relational) is your child active? In what areas is he passive?

- The rule of thumb here is, "You don't get the goodies until you make real efforts in your problem area(s)."

Session Seven: *Boundary Principles Nine and Ten* 141

Guided by this rule, what is one step you will take this week to help your child get beyond his passivity in certain areas? Be specific.

Laziness

Sometimes kids are passive because they have little "anticipatory anxiety." The future holds no fear for them. They know someone else will take care of any problems that arise. They lack fear of consequences.

- At the root of most lazy kids lies an enabling parent. Kids will be as passive as you train them to be. What degree of passivity are you allowing? To answer that question, ask yourself whether running the household is a team effort or a token effort on your children's parts. Is their income tied to performance at home and school? If not, how could it be incorporated?

- What would another parent say about your expectations of your kid? Ask! Find out whether another parent thinks you're doing too much and your child too little.

- Set limits and consequences for laziness today. Outline them here and schedule a time for explaining them to your child.

---

142 *Boundaries with Kids Participant's Guide*

Entitlement

A major cause of passivity in children is an entitled attitude, a demand for special treatment. Such children feel they deserve to be served by virtue of their existence. In fact, all kids have a certain amount of entitlement.

- God's solution for entitlement is humility (Philippians 2:3). What will you do this week to temper your child by frustrating his grandiose feelings while still satisfying his real needs?

- To counter your child's sense of entitlement, don't go overboard praising required behavior. But do go overboard when your child confesses the truth, repents honestly, takes chances, and loves openly. In light of this guideline, what events from the past week would you handle differently in the future? What changes in your standard responses to your child—if any—will you make in light of this guideline?

Clinical Issues

- Sometimes childhood passivity can be a symptom of an underlying emotional disorder or of drug and alcohol problems. If you suspect these issues, what will you do to find a therapist experienced with kids your child's age so you can get a clinical opinion?

Session Seven: *Boundary Principles Nine and Ten* 143

The Law of Exposure

Even the most verbal kids and parents can benefit from the following principles for safe communication.

1. All feelings are acceptable, and expressing feelings is a good thing.

2. Expression of these feelings, however, has certain limits. For example, "I am angry with you" is okay, but "You are an idiot" is not okay. Hitting and throwing things are not okay either.

3. Empathize first to make a connection. First contain, accept, and love the children's feelings, then seek to understand.

4. Self-control is the most important element. Children are out of control at this point, and they need your structure.

5. Guard against splitting your love and limits. Be kind and loving, but remain strong enough to let them know that their feelings have not destroyed you or driven you away.

6. Leave your pride, ego, and narcissism somewhere else. Reactions from those parts of you will reinforce your children's most primitive fears.

7. After the conflict, have some good bonding time, even if it is just communicating affection. This lets them know the connection is secure even in conflict.

8. Put words with feelings. Children are responsible for their feelings; putting words to feelings adds structure to them and keeps them smaller than ultimate reality. If we can name and explain our feelings, they are just

---

144 *Boundaries with Kids Participant's Guide*

feelings, not global realities. Feeling sad is different from feeling as if the world is ending.

9. Keep lessons out of the interaction until you know your children have dealt with their feelings. Otherwise, they will not be listening.

10. The main guiding principle is this: "Our relationship is bigger than this conflict, feeling, or experience. Our connection and affection will remain after this conflict is past."

- Schedule a time during this week to talk through some or all of the principles for safe communication. Let your kids offer their opinions and ask questions about how to live them out in real life. The family discussion might end with choosing one principle to focus on as a family this week.

- Before the next meeting, take a few minutes to review the ten laws we looked at over the last five weeks. Identify an area or two that you want to work on. In our final meeting next week, we'll be looking at six steps to implementing these boundaries with your kids.

BETWEEN SESSIONS READING

"Jump-starting My Engine: The Law of Activity" and "Honesty Is the Best Policy: The Law of Exposure," chapters 12 and 13 in *Boundaries with Kids*.

Session Eight

Six Steps to Implementing Boundaries with Your Kids

BEFORE YOU LEAD

Key Points

- Boundaries with kids isn't about "making" your child do anything.

- Boundaries with kids is much more about structuring your child's existence so that he experiences the consequences of his behavior, thus leading him to be more responsible and caring.

- The six steps are:

  1. See the three realities.

  2. Plug in.

  3. Grow in boundaries personally.

  4. Evaluate and plan.

  5. Present the plan.

  6. Follow through over time.

- We cannot overemphasize how critical it is to stick with the consequences. Your consequence is a team effort by you and God for lovingly nurturing and training your child.

- It is never too late to start boundary training.

- Don't ever give up on your children. You are the only mom or dad they will ever have; no one in the world is in the position of influence in their heart that you are.

- God is the ultimate resource for your parenting, so turn to him. Consistently read and study his Word so you'll gain or strengthen a structure for your life and your parenting. After all, life works better for us when we do it God's way.

- God designed your child with a need to learn to take ownership of his life in submission to him. Your child may not be aware of that need, but you are. As a parent, you are helping to develop the image of God within your child that is already there and waiting to be strengthened (Genesis 1:27).

Synopsis

Boundaries with kids isn't about "making" your child do anything. It is about structuring your child's existence so he experiences the consequences of his behavior, thus leading him to be more responsible and caring. Keep that in mind as you review these six steps to implementing boundaries with your kids.

The first step is to *see the three realities*. First, there really is a problem: our child is not perfect. Second, the problem isn't really the problem. It is the symptom of another issue, which in many cases is a boundary problem. And, third, time does *not* heal all.

The second step is to *plug in*. Connect to good, supportive relationships in addition to your spouse. Get with people who make it politically incorrect *not* to have kid problems. You'll come out relieved that you aren't nuts and that there is hope.

The third step is to *grow in boundaries personally*. It's hard for kids to grow when they aren't around growing parents.

The fourth step is to *evaluate and plan*. Evaluate your child's situation and your resources, and develop a plan to deal with the problem.

The fifth step is to *present the plan* and invite your child to partner with you. The key is that, if she chooses to resist, the consequences will become a reality.

The sixth step is to *follow through over time*. You need to do what you say you will do. Here are some of the things with which you may have to deal:

- Expect disbelief and testing.

- Be patient and allow repeated trials.

- Praise the child's adaptations.

- Fine-tune and shift issues.

Is it ever too late to start this kind of boundary training? We would say that it is never too late to begin doing the right thing for your child and you.

Don't give up on your children, even in the last years of adolescence. You are the only mom or dad they will ever have. No one in the world is in the position of influence in their heart that you are.

Whatever your situation as a parent, God has anticipated it, is fully aware of it, and wants to help you to help your child develop boundaries. He has provided hope for your future and your child's future that is real and helpful. God is the ultimate resource for your parenting, so turn to him. God's people can also offer various kinds of support—prayers and perspective, advice and counsel.

And, finally, remember that God designed your child with a need to learn to take ownership of his life in submission to God. Your child may not be aware of that need—but you are. And as a parent, you are helping to develop the image of God within your child that is already there and waiting to be strengthened (Genesis 1:27).

Session Outline (56 minutes)

 I. Introduction (10 minutes)
    A. Welcome (1 minute)
    B. Review and Overview (8 minutes)
    C. Opening Prayer (1 minute)
 II. Discovery (38 minutes)
    A. Video Segment: Roll Up Your Sleeves, Part 1 (7 minutes)
    B. Kid Talk: Get Ready! Get Set! (8 minutes)
    C. Kid Kare: Implementing Boundaries: Steps 1–3 (5 minutes)
    D. Video Segment: Roll Up Your Sleeves, Part 2 (4 minutes)
    E. Kid Talk: Running the Race (6 minutes)
    F. Kid Kare: Implementing Boundaries: Steps 4–6 (5 minutes)
    G. Video Segment: Words of Hope and Encouragement (3 minutes)
 III. Wrap-up (8 minutes)

Recommended Reading

"Roll Up Your Sleeves: The Six Steps to Implementing Boundaries with Your Kids," chapter 14 in *Boundaries with Kids*.

Session Eight

Six Steps to Implementing Boundaries with Your Kids

10 MINUTES INTRODUCTION

1 minute — Welcome

> Call the group together and welcome the participants to Session 8: Six Steps to Implementing Boundaries with Your Kids.

8 minutes — Review and Overview

> Participant's Guide page 145.

So how was your week? It would be great to hear about how you worked on turning passivity into activity and what you did to improve direct communication in your family.

> Note: Based on your knowledge of the participants and time available, choose from among the following questions. Be ready to provide anecdotes from your own life.

What did you do to encourage, if not require, your kids to take initiative and work at problem solving?

As we encourage our kids to move from passivity to activity, we may find ourselves having to say some tough things. "I'm sorry, but that's your responsibility. I hope you solve your problem; it sounds difficult, but I'm pulling for you." When, if at all, did any of you have the opportunity to say something like that this week? What were the circumstances? What was your child's response?

Who had an opportunity to teach your child to move toward relationship? Describe the situation. What did you say, and how did your son or daughter respond?

136

PLANNING NOTES

_____

_____

_____

_____

_____

_____

_____

_____

_____

_____

_____

_____

_____

_____

_____

_____

_____

_____

_____

_____

_____

_____

_____

_____

_____

Session Eight

Six Steps to Implementing Boundaries with Your Kids

OVERVIEW

In this session, you will

- Be reminded that it is hard for kids to grow when they aren't around growing parents.
- Learn six steps to implementing boundaries with your kids.
- Be warned about four things you'll have to deal with as you take these steps.
- Be charged to follow through with the consequences you establish.

145

What did any of you do to make passivity more painful than activity?

Who consciously chose to model open communication at home this week? Describe the situation.

Who had the opportunity to be more active about pursuing your child's feelings? What did you do?

> Possible answers: Try to ask questions or interpret the silence with statements like "It seems like you are mad/sad right now" and "I think you might be upset with me."

Who worked with their kids on specific boundary words and perhaps even did some role-playing?

I'm glad to hear how you are applying what we have been talking about! As you'll hear from Dr. Cloud and Dr. Townsend in a minute, these eight weeks together have not just been about gaining new information. We hope that you are letting these truths have an impact on your life and on your parenting.

In fact, that's the focus of our session. As the title says, we're going to look at six steps to implementing boundaries with your kids! You'll also be warned about four things you'll have to deal with as you take these steps. you'll be charged to follow through with the consequences you establish. And Dr. Townsend and Dr. Cloud will remind you that it's hard for kids to grow when they aren't around growing parents.

Let's open with a word of prayer.

1 minute	## Opening Prayer

Lord God, thank you for all you have been showing us about ourselves in this class we took to learn more about our kids. Not only have we learned much about kids, but we've also needed to look at ourselves. You've shown us where we need to grow in order to help our kids grow. You've called us, among other things, to learn from the consequences of our own actions, to be respectful, to practice gratitude, and to be honest in our relationships so that we can help our kids do the same. We ask that you would open our hearts and minds once again to your truth. Keep us from being defensive, protect us from thoughts of inadequacy and hopelessness, and make us willing to learn new behaviors so that we implement the boundary principles we've been studying. We pray in Jesus' name. Amen.

38 MINUTES DISCOVERY

3 minutes	### Video Segment: Roll Up Your Sleeves, Part 1

> Remind the participants that key points of the video segment can be found on page 146 of the Participant's Guide if they would like to review them at a later time.

PLANNING NOTES

_____

_____

_____

_____

_____

_____

_____

_____

_____

_____

_____

_____

_____

_____

_____

_____

_____

_____

_____

_____

_____

_____

_____

_____

_____

_____

Session Eight

Six Steps to Implementing Boundaries with Your Kids

OVERVIEW

In this session, you will

- Be reminded that it is hard for kids to grow when they aren't around growing parents.
- Learn six steps to implementing boundaries with your kids.
- Be warned about four things you'll have to deal with as you take these steps.
- Be charged to follow through with the consequences you establish.

145

---

146   *Boundaries with Kids Participant's Guide*

VIDEO SEGMENT

Roll Up Your Sleeves, Part 1

- Boundaries with kids isn't about "making" your child do anything.
- Boundaries with kids is much more about structuring your child's existence so that he experiences the consequences of his behavior, thus leading him to be more responsible and caring.
- The first step to implementing boundaries with your kids is to *see three realities:*

  1. There really is a problem: Your child is not perfect.
  2. The problem isn't really the problem. Whichever of your kids' behaviors and attitudes are driving you crazy isn't the real issue. It is the symptom of another issue, which, in many cases, is a boundary problem.
  3. Time does not heal all.

- The second step is to *plug in.* Connect to good, supportive relationships in addition to your spouse. Such relationships offer you a place to trade tips, secrets, techniques, and victories and failures.
- The third step is to *grow in boundaries personally.* Kids know when you are being a hypocrite or telling them to do something you won't, and it's hard for kids to grow when they aren't around growing parents.
- All of us need to be developing and clarifying our boundaries for life.

View Video Segment: Roll Up Your Sleeves, Part 1

We just heard that boundaries with kids is about structuring your child's existence so that he experiences the consequences of his behavior. That sounds like a tall order, so let's talk about it! Please turn to page 147 in your Participant's Guide.

6 minutes   *Kid Talk: Get Ready! Get Set!*

Participant's Guide page 147.

1. Kids need parents who will *be* boundaries. This means that in whatever situation arises, you will respond to your child with empathy, firmness, freedom, and consequences. Define each of these elements and explain why each is crucial.

2. If you want your farm to run right, it's wise to ask the one who made the farm how to run it. You need all that God has to help you live. What can God give you that will help you raise your kids?

3. Time does not automatically resolve our issues with our kids. Time is only a context for healing; it is not the healing process itself. Infections need more than time; they need antibiotics. What antibiotics have you received from this video series?

This session on how to implement boundaries is full of antibiotics. You'll find some as you look more closely at the first three steps of implementing boundaries. Please turn to pages 151 through 154 of your Participant's Guide.

5 minutes   *Kid Kare: Implementing Boundaries: Steps 1–3*

Participant's Guide pages 148–51.

Directions

Working alone or with your spouse, you'll have 5 minutes to start applying the first three steps for implementing boundaries to your specific situation at home. Any questions?

Let the participants know when there is 1 minute remaining. Call the group back together after 5 minutes.

Having learned the first three steps of implementing boundaries, you're undoubtedly ready for the last three. Let's learn about those now.

PLANNING NOTES

_____

_____

_____

_____

_____

_____

_____

_____

_____

_____

_____

_____

_____

_____

_____

_____

_____

_____

KID TALK

Get Ready! Get Set!

1. Kids need parents who will *be* boundaries. This means that in whatever situation arises, you will respond to your child with empathy, firmness, freedom, and consequences. Define each of these elements and explain why each is crucial.

2. If you want your farm to run right, it's wise to ask the one who made the farm how to run it. You need all that God has to help you live. What can God give you that will help you raise your kids?

3. Time does not automatically resolve our issues with our kids. Time is only a context for healing; it is not the healing process itself. Infections need more than time; they need antibiotics. What antibiotics have you received from this video series?

KID KARE

Implementing Boundaries: Steps 1–3

DIRECTIONS

Working alone or with your spouse, you'll have 5 minutes to start applying the first three steps for implementing boundaries to your specific situation at home.

Step 1: See the Three Realities

First, there really is a problem: Your child is not perfect.

1. What evidence do you see of this reality? Be honest with yourself about your child.

2. With what aspects of your child's behavior (if any) are you rationalizing genuine problems and playing the semantics game as you describe unacceptable actions and attitudes? Is smarting off "a cute sense of humor," laziness "fatigue," or intrusiveness "high-spiritedness"?

3. What honest friend will you consult if you are struggling to see your child's shortcomings?

Second, come to grips with the fact that the problem isn't really the problem. The behavior or attitude driving you crazy isn't the real issue. It is the symptom of another issue, which in many cases is a boundary problem. Bad grades, for instance, are not the real problem; lack of concern about consequences is. Being controlling of other kids is not the real problem; lack of respect for other

---

people's boundaries is. Your child's inattention to instructions is not the real problem; lack of fear of consequences is.

4. What, if anything, do these examples suggest about the issues you are dealing with in your home?

5. Consider too any crises you have weathered recently. What might the behaviors you've identified suggest about your child? What is your next step in pursuing the root of the problem and helping him start developing boundaries?

Third, understand that time does not heal all. Time is only a context for healing; it is not the healing process itself. Infections need more than time; they need antibiotics.

6. In what current parenting situation are you merely hoping that time alone will resolve it? What course of action—if any that you're aware of—are you wanting to avoid?

Step 2: Plug In

When you begin to address the problems you see in your child and get involved in the repair process, make sure you connect to good, supportive relationships in addition to your spouse. Such relationships offer you a place to trade tips, secrets, techniques, and victories and failures. So get with people who make it politically incorrect *not* to have kid problems. You'll come out relieved that you aren't nuts and that there is hope.

1. Whom have you found who won't condemn you, who will walk with you through the fire, and who will hold you accountable

---

to do the right thing? When has that person's support helped you stick to your guns with your kids? Give an example.

2. If you don't have such people in your life yet, what can you do about finding or starting a parenting group, a Bible study that works on boundary issues, a neighborhood group, or finding someone to meet with one-on-one?

Step 3: Grow in Boundaries Personally

Before you start preaching boundaries to your child, start walking the walk. Kids are able to sense deception amazingly well. They know when you are being a hypocrite or telling them to do something you won't do yourself. But even more than that, we could all use work on developing and clarifying our boundaries for life.

1. In general, how well do you maintain healthy boundaries? What are you currently doing to grow in boundaries?

2. Review the Ten Laws of Boundaries. Which laws could you be working on?

3. What, if anything, have your kids said or done that suggests they aren't seeing *your* boundaries at work in your own life even though you are wanting *them* to develop boundaries?

---

4. It is hard for kids to grow when they aren't around growing parents. What are you currently doing to grow spiritually, emotionally, and in good character? If your list seems too short, what will you do to start growing spiritually, emotionally, and in good character?

4 minutes   *Video Segment: Roll Up Your Sleeves, Part 2*

> Remind the participants that key points of the video segment can be found on page 152 of the Participant's Guide if they would like to review them at a later time.

> View Video Segment: Roll Up Your Sleeves, Part 2.

We've heard about all six of the steps involved in implementing boundaries with kids. Let's step back and consider what we can do to create an environment that will encourage boundary development.

6 minutes   *Kid Talk: Running the Race*

> Participant's Guide page 153.

1. In the video, Dr. Cloud suggested taking a "for" stance instead of an "against" stance. We should let our children know that this process isn't about forcing them to do something or because you're angry. Instead, tell your child that you want to deal with a particular issue because you love her, and you want to deal with it together with her. Let's role-play this right now. Who would like to practice stating a problem you're facing with your child?

> If no one volunteers, propose one of the following: chores, an attitude problem, homework, or conflict with a sibling.

2. When you see growth in your child, why is it important to not focus on your love for her when you're validating her efforts?

> Possible answers: You don't want your child sensing she has to earn your love. Your conditional love is not an accurate representation of God's love for her. You want her to be totally confident that you'll always love her even if you don't like her behavior.

3. As you work on implementing these six steps for growth over the long term, what can you do to be sure that your child doesn't feel that your whole relationship is about boundaries?

> Possible answers: Make time to have fun together. Consciously choose topics of conversation that have nothing to do with boundaries. Find a project (craft, service, ministry, etc.) that you can do together.

PLANNING NOTES

_____

_____

_____

_____

_____

_____

_____

_____

_____

_____

_____

_____

_____

_____

_____

_____

_____

_____

_____

_____

_____

_____

_____

_____

152　　*Boundaries with Kids Participant's Guide*

VIDEO SEGMENT
Roll Up Your Sleeves, Part 2

- The fourth step in boundary implementation is to *evaluate and plan*. Evaluate your child's situation and your resources and develop a plan to deal with the problem.

- The fifth step is to *present the plan* and invite your child to partner with you. Present the problem, your expectations, and the consequences as clearly and specifically as possible. Negotiate what is negotiable. Stay in control of what is yours and encourage her freedom to choose. The key is that, if she chooses to resist, the consequences will become a reality.

- The sixth step is to *follow through over time*. The plan will fall apart if you are not personally functioning as the boundary for your child. Be sure to do what you say you will do.

- Here are some of the things with which you may need to deal while implementing boundaries:

    Expect disbelief and testing.

    Be patient and allow repeated trials.

    Praise the child's adaptations.

    Fine-tune and shift issues.

- We cannot overemphasize how critical it is to stick with the consequences. Your consequence is a team effort by you and God for lovingly nurturing and training your child.

Session Eight: *Implementing Boundaries with Your Kids*　　153

KID TALK
Running the Race

1. In the video, Dr. Cloud suggested taking a "for" stance instead of an "against" stance. We should let our children know that this process isn't about forcing them to do something or because you're angry. Instead, tell your child that you want to deal with a particular issue because you love her, and you want to deal with it together with her. Let's role-play this right now. Who would like to practice stating a problem you're facing with your child?

2. When you see growth in your child, why is it important to not focus on your love for her when you're validating her efforts?

3. As you work on implementing these six steps for growth over the long term, what can you do to be sure that your child doesn't feel that your whole relationship is about boundaries?

Please turn to pages 154 through 161 of your Participant's Guide.

5 minutes ## Kid Kare: Implementing Boundaries: Steps 4–6

> Participant's Guide pages 154–61.

Directions

For this exercise, take 5 minutes, alone or with your spouse, to start applying these steps to the parenting challenges you currently face. Any questions?

> Let the participants know when there is 1 minute remaining. Call the group back together after 5 minutes.

Well, Dr. Cloud and Dr. Townsend have outlined six steps of implementing boundaries, but they're definitely not six simple steps that are done quickly once. Appropriately enough, they have words of hope and encouragement for you. So, before we close with prayer, let's hear one final time from Dr. Cloud and Dr. Townsend.

3 minutes ## Video Segment: Words of Hope and Encouragement

> Remind the participants that key points of the video segment can be found on page 162 of the Participant's Guide if they would like to review them at a later time.

> View Video Segment: Words of Hope and Encouragement.

8 MINUTES ## WRAP-UP

> Participant's Guide pages 163–64.

You'll notice a few Kid Kare at Home items on pages 167 and 168 of your Participant's Guide. Now let's close in prayer. At one point I will prompt you to pray specifically for your children. You can do so out loud or silently. Either way, please use this time to lay your concerns for your kids before the Lord, their Creator, their Great Physician, the Redeemer, your Rock, and your heavenly Father.

---

154   *Boundaries with Kids Participant's Guide*

KID KARE

Implementing Boundaries: Steps 4–6

DIRECTIONS

For this exercise, take 5 minutes, alone or with your spouse, to start applying these steps to the parenting challenges you currently face.

Step 4: Evaluate and Plan

Your child

Evaluate your child's situation and your resources, and develop a plan to deal with the problem.

1. Get to know your child's boundary problem in light of herself. If you haven't done so already, list the following important factors:
   - *Age:* What issues are normal for your child's age-group? What is she capable of? At what point are you pushing her beyond her comfort level (a good thing), but not beyond her abilities?

   - *Maturity level:* As to the matter of attachment, is your child able to connect emotionally to you? Does she see you as someone who cares for her? Or is she detached, distant, or chronically cold? When it comes to honesty, does your child tell the truth or does she struggle with lying and deceit?

   You can also gauge maturity level by considering such fundamental issues as:

   Basic trust

   Ability to make and keep good friends

Session Eight: *Implementing Boundaries with Your Kids*   155

Responsiveness to commands

Ability to disagree and protest

Ability to tolerate deprivation

Ability to accept loss and failure in herself and others

Attitude toward authority

Which of these are you concerned about? What events or behavioral patterns have given rise to that concern?

- *Context:* What is the setting for your child's life? Are you divorced, or is your marriage in trouble? Does your child have any clinical issues (neurological, learning disorders, attention deficit disorder)? Are there problems with other siblings? What environmental influences affect her?

- *Specific boundary conflict:* What is the specific boundary issue in your child's life? Is she having problems with family rules, chores, school, or friends? State the issue as simply as possible.

- *Severity:* How profound is the problem you just specified? Be sure that you're not sweating the small stuff. Address issues that involve honesty, responsibility, caring, and morality. Give more latitude within limits to hairstyle, music, and room sloppiness.

---

156   *Boundaries with Kids Participant's Guide*

Yourself

2. Now that you are getting a more comprehensive picture of your child's boundary problem, where it comes from, and how severe it is, evaluate what you have at hand to deal with it. Look at the following factors:
   - *Your own issues.* What have you seen about how you react and interact with your child? What causes you to respond inappropriately? What are you doing to grow in that area?

   - *Your life context.* Where, if at all, is there chaos or crisis in your life? What do you need to do to get in a position where you have enough order and structure to bring order and structure to your child? If you're a single parent, where are you finding the help and resources you need to deal with your child's boundary problems? Check with your community, church, neighborhood, relatives, and friends for assistance.

   - *A boundary-resistant spouse.* Are you dealing with a boundary-resistant spouse? If so, are you—as the "pro-boundaries" and therefore the "mean" and "depriving" one—caught in the middle between your spouse and your child? What can you do to rearrange things so that the boundaryless parent reaps the consequences of his or her irresponsibility? See this as not a parenting issue but as a marriage issue. What are you doing to address the marriage issues caused by boundarylessness?

Session Eight: *Implementing Boundaries with Your Kids*   157

The plan

3. Come up with a structure that you will use for yourself and will present to the child. Include the following aspects and write them down:
   - *The problem.* State the problem as specifically as possible. Stay away from character attacks that the child would have to defend herself against.

   - *The expectations.* Make your expectations specific and measurable.

   - *The consequences.* Write what will happen when the child doesn't meet your expectations. Set it up so that, as much as possible, the punishment fits the crime. Set up positive consequences too, for success in meeting expectations, but don't go overboard in reinforcing anything that's above savage-level behavior.

Step 5: Present the Plan

The more you involve your child in the boundary-setting and boundary-honoring process and the more time, help, and information she gets, the more likely she is to take ownership of it and cooperate in her own growth. Invite your partner with you, even though the plan is still going to be executed if she refuses.

1. Introduce the plan at a peaceful time. What time and place will be good for you and your child? If that moment comes and you're not getting along, wait for another time.

---

158   *Boundaries with Kids Participant's Guide*

2. Take a "for" stance instead of an "against" stance. What will you say to communicate that you see a problem that's hurting her and others in her life, that you want to deal with it because you love her, and that you want to work with her?

3. Present the problem. What specific hurtful effects of the behavior in focus will you talk about?

4. Present the expectations. What specific standards will you set forth?

5. Present the consequences. What specific consequences will you establish? Know exactly what your plan is so that you can communicate clearly and directly.

6. Negotiate what is negotiable. Ask your child for input, within parameters, on the expectations and consequences of your plan. Where can you give a little in those categories? What points are nonnegotiable? What will you say if she asks, "You don't do that. Why should I?"

Session Eight: *Implementing Boundaries with Your Kids*   159

7. Make expectations and consequences easily accessible. What will you do to remind your child of the expectations and consequences? Where, for instance, could you post them?

Step 6: Follow Through over Time

Expect disbelief and testing

Although your child may argue with you when you present the plan, it is when you enforce the consequence after she transgresses the boundary that you will see the resistance.

1. You can expect reactions like shock, disbelief, anger, expressions of hurt and woundedness, isolation, blaming, attempts to pit you against the other parent, and even escalation of the behavior. Which of these do you expect your child to choose? How do you want to respond?

2. What feelings do you expect to have when your child resists the consequences? What will you do to enforce the consequences? Whom do you have supporting you so you can stay with it?

3. When has a lack of structure and consequences cost you? Or when has being overcontrolled, with no ability to choose, kept you handicapped in making decisions? Let these experiences help you stick to the consequences and not protect your child from reality, from the consequences of her actions.

---

160   *Boundaries with Kids Participant's Guide*

Be patient and allow repeated trials

Your child is on a learning curve, and learning takes many trials. Expect her not only to transgress the boundary but also to protest the consequences many times.

4. What will you do to maintain an appropriate level of patience with your child—and with yourself?

5. If you find yourself having trouble with consistently enforcing boundaries, what mature friends could help you explore whether the problem is one of resources, abilities, character, or unrealistic expectations?

Praise the child's adaptations

If the process works correctly, you will begin to see less of the bad behavior and more of the good behavior you're after.

6. Why is it important to not focus your love for your child when you're validating her efforts? (Hint: Is your love conditional on her efforts? You may have talked about this in your group.)

7. What benefits of her new behavior will you help her see? Look for benefits to others as well as benefits to herself.

Session Eight: *Implementing Boundaries with Your Kids*   161

Fine-tune and shift issues

When you feel the child is mastering the behavior and is more in control of herself, you may want to increase expectations. Or you may want to focus on another problem.

8. What might those increased expectations or that new focus be?

9. What will you do to be sure that your child doesn't feel that your whole relationship is about boundaries? (Again, you may have gotten some ideas from other people in your class.)

10. Your child needs to know that growing up continues all the way through life. What is she seeing in the way you live to reinforce that fact?

We cannot overemphasize how critical it is to stick with the consequences. Remember that every time God disciplines us for our own good, we protest, hate him, whine, shake our fist, and condemn him as being an unfair God. Yet he loves us enough not to let us call the shots and further ruin ourselves. Your consequence is a team effort by you and God for lovingly nurturing and training your child.

---

162   *Boundaries with Kids Participant's Guide*

VIDEO SEGMENT

Words of Hope and Encouragement

- Is it ever too late to start this kind of boundary training? We would say that it is never too late to begin doing the right thing for your child and you. You can always, for instance, start becoming more honest and clearer about responsibility; taking more initiative to solve problems; and bringing a sense of structure to your home—whatever your kids' ages.

- Don't give up on your children, even in the last years of adolescence. You are the only mom or dad they will ever have. No one in the world is in the position of influence in their heart that you are.

- Whatever your situation as a parent, God has anticipated it, is fully aware of it, and wants to help you to help your child develop boundaries. God is the ultimate resource for your parenting, so turn to him. Consistently read and study his Word so you'll gain or strengthen a structure for your life and your parenting. After all, life works better for us when we do it God's way.

- God's people can also offer various kinds of support—prayers and perspective, advice and counsel.

- Remember that God designed your child with a need to learn to take ownership of his life in submission to God. Your child may not be aware of that need—but you are. As a parent, you are helping to develop the image of God within your child that is already there and waiting to be strengthened (Genesis 1:27).

Closing Prayer

Lord God, in your Word you tell us that "He who began a good work in you will see it through to completion"! That's a promise that gives us such encouragement right now because we are well aware of the work you have started in our lives and the lives of our kids over these past eight weeks. Hear us, Lord, as we pray—silently or aloud— for our kids and ourselves. . . .

> Allow 5–8 minutes for group members to pray aloud or silently.

Lord, please continue the work you have begun in us and in our kids. We ask you to pour your grace into our families, the grace of patience and perseverance, wisdom and strength for us parents; the grace of openness and teachability for our kids; and the grace of love and humility in our relationships with one another. To God be the glory for the loving work of transformation you have done and are doing! We pray in Jesus' name. Amen.

PLANNING NOTES

_____

_____

_____

_____

_____

_____

_____

_____

_____

_____

_____

_____

_____

_____

_____

_____

_____

_____

_____

_____

_____

_____

_____

_____

_____

_____

Closing Prayer

Lord God, in your Word you tell me that "He who began a good work in you will see it through to completion"! That's a promise that gives me such encouragement right now because I am well aware of the work you have started in my life and the lives of my kids over these past eight weeks. Hear me, Lord, as I pray for my kids and myself. . . .

Lord, please continue the work you have begun in me and in my kids. I ask you to pour your grace into my family, the grace of patience and perseverance, wisdom and strength for me as a parent; the grace of openness and teachability for my kids; and the grace of love and humility in my relationships with others. To God be the glory for the loving work of transformation you have done and are doing! I pray in Jesus' name. Amen.

Kid Kare at Home

1. So that you can thoughtfully implement boundaries with your kids, finish the Kid Kare exercises you began in this final session. Then follow the six steps outlined in this session for boundary implementation. Structure your child's existence so that he experiences the consequences of his behavior, thus leading him to be more responsible and caring.

2. Stay connected. Find the support you need in the Lord, his Word, and his people.

3. Keep praying! God is the ultimate resource for your parenting, so turn to him continually (1 Thessalonians 5:17).

LAST SESSION READING

"Six Steps to Implementing Boundaries with Your Kids," chapter 14 in *Boundaries with Kids*.

Embark on a Life-Changing Journey of Personal and Spiritual Growth

DR. HENRY CLOUD   **DR. JOHN TOWNSEND**

Dr. Henry Cloud and Dr. John Townsend have been bringing hope and healing to millions for over two decades. They have helped people everywhere discover solutions to life's most difficult personal and relational challenges. Their material provides solid, practical answers and offers guidance in the areas of *parenting, singles issues, personal growth,* and *leadership.*

Bring either Dr. Cloud or Dr. Townsend to your church or organization. They are available for:

- Seminars on a wide variety of topics
- Training for small group leaders
- Conferences
- Educational events
- Consulting with your organization

Other opportunities to experience Dr. Cloud and Dr. Townsend:

- Ultimate Leadership workshops—held in Southern California throughout the year
- Small group curriculum
- Seminars via Satellite
- Solutions Audio Club—Solutions is a weekly recorded presentation

For other resources, and for dates of seminars and workshops
by Dr. Cloud and Dr. Townsend, visit:
www.cloudtownsend.com

For other information **Call (800) 676-HOPE (4673)**

Or write to:
Cloud-Townsend Resources
3176 Pullman Street, Suite 105
Costa Mesa, CA

About the Writer

Lisa Guest has been writing, editing, and developing curriculum since 1984. She holds a Master's Degree in English Literature from UCLA and teaches at her church whenever the opportunity arises. She lives in Irvine, California, with her husband and three children.

Other ZondervanGroupware™ Products Available by Drs. Henry Cloud and John Townsend

Boundaries
When to Say Yes, When to Say No, to Take Control of Your Life

Based on the best-selling, award-winning book, this 9-session curriculum teaches the basics of developing healthy boundaries in order to maintain healthy relationships. It is designed for use with groups of all sizes.

This resource kit contains:
- 1 120-minute video
- 1 Leader's guide
- 1 Participant's Guide
- 1 *Boundaries* softcover book

ISBN 0-310-22362-8

Boundaries in Marriage
An 8-Session Focus on Boundaries and Marriage

Based on the book, this 8-session curriculum will encourage the kind of spiritual and emotional growth and character development that enables marriage—within God's boundaries—to be fun, spiritually fulfilling, and growth producing.

This resource kit contains:
- 1 105-minute video & DVD included— use either one
- 1 Leader's guide
- 1 Participant's guide
- 1 *Boundaries in Marriage* softcover book

ISBN 0-310-24612-1

Pick up a copy today at your favorite bookstore!

Boundaries in Dating

Making Dating Work

All the immense value of the book is available in this complete 10-session curriculum kit for groups of any size. It will encourage spiritual and emotional growth and character development that enables dating—within God's boundaries—to be fun, spiritually fulfilling, and growth producing.

This resource kit contains:
- 1 120-minute video
- 1 Leader's guide
- 1 Participant's guide
- 1 *Boundaries in Dating* softcover book

ISBN 0-310-23873-0

Raising Great Kids for Parents of Preschoolers

A Comprehensive Guide to Parenting with Grace and Truth

From the authors of *Boundaries,* comes this complete 6-session curriculum kit for groups of all sizes. It will empower parents of preschoolers to become more intentional and effective in their parenting, enabling them to raise great kids starting now with their zero to five-year-olds.

This resource kit contains:
- 1 120-minute video
- 1 Leader's guide
- 1 Participant's guide
- 1 *Raising Great Kids* softcover book

ISBN 0-310-23238-4

Pick up a copy today at your favorite bookstore!

**Understanding the Biblical Process of Growth to Help People
Move into Christ-like Maturity**

How People Grow
*What the Bible Reveals about
Personal Growth*

Dr. Henry Cloud and
Dr. John Townsend

Does Christianity really work? Why do many sincere Christians fail to make progress in some areas of their lives even though they work hard to apply the spiritual solutions they have been taught? They learn about God's love, yet continue to feel depressed. They understand the crucified life, but still struggle with problems in their relationships. They focus on their security in Christ, but continue to overeat. "Spiritual interventions" are not working for them.

In this foundational work, Cloud and Townsend describe the principles they use in their private practice, in their teaching and semi-nars, and in their writing of books like *Boundaries, Changes That Heal,* and *Safe People*. Their practical approach to helping people grow really works and has such transforming power in people's lives because their principles are grounded in both orthodox Christian faith and a keen understanding of human nature. This book will be useful both to those who are helping people grow spiritually, as well as to those who are seeking growth themselves.

Hardcover 0-310-22153-6
Audio Pages® Abridged Cassettes 0-310-24065-4
Workbook 0-310-24569-9

Boundaries with Kids

Boundaries with Kids helps parents apply the Ten Laws of Boundaries (first described in *Boundaries*) to the challenges of raising children. In their popular, readable style, Cloud and Townsend help moms and dads make choices and develop a parenting approach that sees beyond the moment to the adults their children will become.

Hardcover 0-310-20035-0
Softcover 0-310-24315-7
Audio Pages® Abridged Cassettes 0-310-20456-9
Workbook 0-310-22349-0

Boundaries in Dating
Making Dating Work

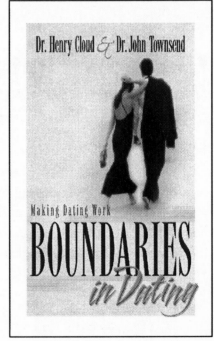

Between singleness and marriage lies the journey of dating. Want to make your road as smooth as possible? Set and maintain healthy boundaries—boundaries that will help you grow in freedom, honesty, and self-control.

Softcover 0-310-20034-2
Audio Pages® Abridged Cassettes 0-310-20455-0
Workbook 0-310-23330-5
Zondervan*Groupware*™ 0-310-23873-0
Leader's Guide 0-310-23874-9
Participant's Guide 0-310-23875-7

Pick up a copy today at your favorite bookstore!

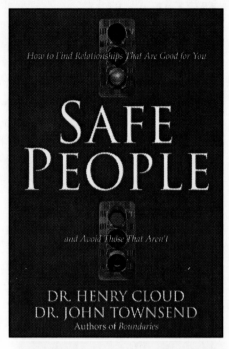

Hiding From Love

How to Change the Withdrawal Patterns That Isolate and Imprison You

Dr. John Townsend

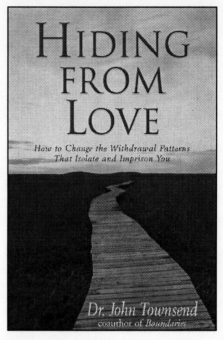

Hiding From Love helps you to explore the hiding patterns you've developed in dealing with your emotions and guides you toward the healing grace and truth that God has built into safe, connected relationships.

Softcover 0-310-20107-1
Workbook 0-310-23828-5

The Mom Factor

Discover how to:
- Transform the Effects of the Past
- Say "No" to Your Mom Without Feeling Guilty
- Build a Healthy Relationship with Your Mom
- Improve All Your Relationships!

Softcover 0-310-22559-0

12 "Christian" Beliefs That Can Drive You Crazy

Relief from False Assumptions

Not everything believed to be a biblical truth is truly biblical. The authors debunk twelve commonly accepted beliefs that cause bondage rather than liberty.

Softcover 0-310-49491-5

We want to hear from you. Please send your comments about this book to us in care of zreview@zondervan.com. Thank you.